CHRISTOPHER SMART

CHRISTOPHER SMART

selected poems

edited by
Marcus Walsh

Fyfield Books
Carcanet · Manchester

ACKNOWLEDGEMENTS

For permission to reprint 'On Gratitude: To the Memory of Mr Seaton', the manuscript of which is in the Henry W. and Albert A. Berg Collection, I am grateful to the New York Public Library, Astor, Lenox and Tilden Foundations; and to Dr Robert Brittain and the Princeton University Press. For permission to base my selection of passages from *Jubilate Agno* on the edition by W. H. Bond (London: Hart-Davis and Cambridge: Harvard University Press, 1954), I am grateful to Dr Bond and Granada Publishing Ltd.

I should like to thank Dr J. W. Binns and Dr R. Wilcher of Birmingham University for their helpful expertise.

M. W.

First published by Carcanet Press Ltd 1972
Revised edition published 1979 by
Carcanet New Press Limited
330 Corn Exchange Buildings
Manchester M4 3BG

The publisher acknowledges the financial assistance of the Arts Council of Great Britain.

Printed in England by Billings, Guildford.

CONTENTS

INTRODUCTION

DONALD DAVIE, in his collection of eighteenth-century verse, *The Late Augustans* (London: Heinemann, 1958), has argued: 'It is not impossible that when Smart is judged over the whole range of his various production . . . he will be thought of as the greatest English poet between Pope and Wordsworth' (p. xxviii). This is a reasonable claim: but only recently has criticism begun the close investigation and accurate assessment which will confirm it. Smart is a remarkable phenomenon, a major poet who had almost no impact on his contemporaries, and who has been radically misunderstood for little short of two centuries. A learned man and a genius, he wrote a poetry of conscious and coherent artistry, distinctively his own, accessibly beautiful, often difficult. Great art requires effort from its audience; too much aware of biographical factors, the anecdotage of Smart's personal history, and too disturbed by unfamiliar elements in his work, readers in Smart's own time and later have shrunk from that rewarding labour, and more easily mis-labelled him a mad-poet, or a visionary.

Christopher Smart was born in April 1722, the son of Peter Smart, steward on the Vane family's Kent estates. He attended Durham Grammar School from his father's death in 1733, and went up to Pembroke College, Cambridge, in 1739. He spent the next ten years at Cambridge, pursuing an outstanding and visibly successful career as a scholar and a poet. In 1740, 1741 and 1742 he was selected to write the Tripos Verses, and in 1742 was awarded, in open competition, the Craven Scholarship, which entitled him to adopt the title of Scholar of the University. He was elected to a Fellowship at Pembroke in 1745. Less officially, he busied himself with humorous, amatory and occasional verse, a taste for fine clothes, and a habit of heavy drinking. He was arrested for debt in 1747, and had to be rescued by his friends and colleagues. Partly to escape his debts, partly to leave behind what seemed to him a claustrophobic academic life, he left Cambridge in 1749 for the life of a professional writer in London, where he had literary friends. In 1750 he was introduced by Charles Burney, the musician, to the bookseller John Newbery, for whom he worked until 1755 or 1756. He wrote in, and edited,

Newbery's *Student* (1750-51) and *Midwife* (1750-53), in these and
other periodicals publishing a considerable quantity of light verse
whose panache and urbanity invite comparison with Matthew Prior.
Smart's major independent volume at this time was *Poems on Several
Occasions*, published by subscription in 1752. It contained able and
often witty pieces of an essentially conventional kind; a georgic on
beer-production called 'The Hop-Garden', lyrics, ballads and odes,
many of which had already appeared in the magazines. How far 'the
ingenious Mr Smart', as he was then called, had become an accepted
and well-regarded member of the artistic world is indicated by the
subscription-list, which includes the names of the musicians Thomas
Arne and William Boyce, of Roubiliac the sculptor, of Samuel
Richardson, of William Collins, even of Voltaire. Part of Smart's
efforts in these years was spent in competing for the Seatonian Prize
of Cambridge University with his poems on the Attributes of the
Supreme Being. He was awarded the prize from its inception in 1750
to 1755, failing only in 1754, when he did not enter. This, Smart's
first important venture into purely religious poetry, brought him
some prestige, and provided a small addition to his various and
unreliable sources of income, particularly valuable as he had married,
in 1752, Anna Maria Carnan, Newbery's step-daughter. Illness, and
the financial responsibility of a family, made Smart's affairs more
precarious, and increasingly he was forced into literary slavery,
including a prose translation of Horace (1755), which was to become
a standard school-text. He also signed a notorious ninety-nine year
contract with the bookseller Gardner to write for a periodical called
the *Universal Visiter*.

What had seemed the beginnings of a successful if not strikingly
unusual poetic career were disintegrating with his mental health. His
insanity took the form of apparent religious mania, a literal under-
standing of the Pauline injunction to 'pray without ceasing'. Samuel
Johnson, who helped Smart in this period by doing some writing for
the *Universal Visiter* on his behalf, as always had the just comment:

> Madness frequently discovers itself merely by unnecessary devia-
> tion from the usual modes of the world. My poor friend Smart
> shewed the disturbance of his mind, by falling upon his knees,
> and saying his prayers in the street, or in any other unusual place.

Now although, rationally speaking, it is greater madness not to pray at all, than to pray as Smart did, I am afraid there are so many who do not pray, that their understanding is not called in question. (James Boswell, *The Life of Samuel Johnson*, ed. G. B. Hill, rev. L. F. Powell [Oxford, 1934-50], l. 397)

Smart was to spend the years from 1756 to January 1763 in confinement, in St Luke's Hospital and in private asylums.

It was during this period that Smart began to produce the great religious poetry which is his main claim for our attention, and which this present selection attempts to represent. In 1759 he began the manuscript of *Jubilate Agno*, working on it continuously until he was freed from the madhouse. In the early 1760s, probably in 1762-63, he wrote *A Song to David*, a verse translation of the Psalms, and the *Hymns and Spiritual Songs for the Fasts and Festivals of the Church of England*. He published the *Song* in April, 1763, and the *Psalms* and *Hymns* by subscription in 1765.

These productions, on which Smart had pinned his hopes, were not well received. The early reviewers found them puzzling, and could not resist making pointed references to his illness. William Mason wrote to Thomas Gray that 'I have seen his Song to David & from thence conclude him as mad as ever' (*Correspondence of Thomas Gray*, ed. P. Toynbee and L. Whibley, Oxford: Clarendon Press, 1935, p. 802). Boswell was kinder than most when he spoke of the *Song*, in a letter to Sir David Dalrymple, as 'a very curious composition, being a strange mixture of *dun obscure* and glowing genius at times' (*Letters of James Boswell*, ed. C. B. Tinker, Oxford: Clarendon Press, 1924, p. 39). The *Psalms* were found inferior by the reviewers to James Merrick's rival version, and the superb *Hymns* were noticed in no review whatever. Smart spent the last eight years of his life unrecognised by the literary world and harassed by debt collectors, writing to keep alive and struggling to preserve his poetic identity. He published three small collections of poems in 1763 and 1764, the oratorios *Hannah* and *Abimelech* in 1764 and 1768, and *The Works of Horace, Translated into Verse* in 1767. In the *Poetical Translation of the Fables of Phaedrus* (1764) and *Parables of our Lord and Saviour Jesus Christ* (1768) he wrote for the expanding market in children's literature. Not even so copious an output could save him however from imprisonment for debt. His last collection, the *Hymns for the Amusement of Children* (1770) was written within the Rules of the King's Bench Prison where, in May, 1771, he died.

Despite all the difficulties, Smart produced between 1759 and 1771 not one but several masterpieces: the *Song*, the *Hymns and Spiritual Songs*, the verse Horace, in some respects also the *Jubilate* and *Hymns for the Amusement of Children*. Taken together these works constitute a corpus which, in extent and quality, is equalled by no other poet of the mid-eighteenth century. The transformation from poet of talent to poet of genius was caused not so much by madness wonderfully opening the doors of his perception (the nineteenth-century view of Smart most eminently expressed by Robert Browning in *Parleyings with Certain People of Importance in their Day*, 1887), as by release, in the solitude of the madhouse, from the commercial constraints which had bound him as a hack-writer until 1756.

Some intimations of the nature of the coming achievement may be found in the Seatonian Prize poems. Praising the Creator-God in the verse-form of *Paradise Lost*, and a pseudo-Miltonic language, these pieces are in many aspects of technique and attitude conventional exercises in the eighteenth-century religious sublime, with echoes especially of James Thomson's *The Seasons*. Nonetheless and characteristically this is already a poetry of religious gratitude and adoration, whose central purpose is 'thanks and praise'. In the last of his Seatonian poems, *On the Goodness of the Supreme Being*, Smart handles his difficult medium with some distinction, and most clearly exhorts the world, human and non-human, to the worship of its beneficent maker.

Jubilate Agno is a more original exercise on the theme of praise. It is, or it seems at first to have been intended as, an antiphonal song, an attempt to write a poem in English on the model of Hebrew responsive verse, informed chiefly by Robert Lowth's *De Sacra Poesi Hebraeorum Praelectiones* (1753). This edition follows, in its selection from Fragment B1, the parallel arrangement of 'Let' and 'For' lines established by W. H. Bond. 'Let' verses calling man and the creatures to praise are echoed by more personal and sometimes more imaginative 'For' verses: 'Let Shelumiel rejoice with Olor, who is of a goodly savour, and the very look of him harmonizes the mind./For my existimation is good even amongst the slanderers and my memory shall arise for a sweet savour unto the Lord.' (*Jubilate Agno*, B1.3.) The summoning of animate and inanimate nature to adoration is not so much evidence of religious fanaticism as an attempt to write poetry according to the model of the Psalms:

> Praise the Lord upon earth: ye dragons, and all deeps;
> Fire and hail, snow and vapours: wind and storm fulfilling
> his word;
> Mountains and all hills: fruitful trees and all cedars;
> Beasts and all cattle: worms and feathered fowls.
>
> Psalter 148.7-10

The second vital formal source for the *Jubilate* is the Benedicite, from the Apocryphal Song of the Three Holy Children, and part of the Order for Morning Prayer: 'O all ye Works of the Lord, bless ye the Lord: praise him, and magnify him for ever.' In Smart's understanding, every creature worships God simply by being itself, through its peculiar actions and properties, the 'mazes' of the hare, the 'subtlety and industry' of the spider, the 'piercer' of the flea. The well-known lines on Smart's cat Jeoffry, far from exemplifying a childlike naivety of vision, are an elaborate demonstration of how each closely-observed act may be taken as part of the cat's divine ritual of praise:

> For he is the servant of the Living God duly and daily serving him.
> For at the first glance of the glory of God in the East he worships
> in his way.
>
> B2.698-9

The ravens' 'coarse ruttling' in *On the Goodness of the Supreme Being* is an anticipation of this theme of the particular 'modes of praising', the 'ways of love express' of each of the creatures.

W. F. Stead re-discovered the manuscript of *Jubilate Agno* and published it in 1939, under the title *Rejoice in the Lamb*. It is easy to see why the *Jubilate* has since been a focal point of Smart studies. The poem contains some of Smart's most original and impressive writing, lines in which, more than anywhere else, he sounded a note quite distinct from that of his contemporaries:

> For in my nature I quested for beauty, but God, God hath sent me
> to sea for pearls.   B1.30

For the Sun's at work to make me a garment & the Moon is at
    work for my wife.   B1.111

For GOD the father Almighty plays upon the HARP of stupendous
    magnitude and melody.
For innumerable Angels fly out at every touch and his tune is a
    work of creation.
For at that time malignity ceases and the devils themselves are at
    peace.   B1. 246-8

Jubilate Agno is an extraordinary and sometimes baffling repository
of learning, from such esoteric sources as the cabala, hermeticism and
freemasonry, from the body of received and familiar contemporary
science, or from the expected stock of an accomplished classicist and
philosopher. It began with a serious motive as an experiment towards
a responsive reading of the Anglican church service: 'For it woud be
better if the LITURGY were musically performed.' (B1.252.) Perhaps
also, despite the incompleteness of the surviving manuscript, it is
possible to trace a controlling prophetic scheme, the replacement of
Israel by the English as the chosen race. In Fragment A God is
praised by a chorus of Biblical figures, in Fragment D by English
men and women.

However, for all its lyric quality, for all its learning, and for all the
loftiness of the purpose with which it was begun, *Jubilate Agno* is
not an accomplished work of art. The correspondence of the anti-
phonal lines breaks down in the B Fragment, and the quality of the
writing falls off in the later part of the poem, the richly suggestive
though brief characterisations of the creatures becoming at times little
more than a listing, derived chiefly from Pliny, of species of fishes or
kinds of precious stones. It seems that the *Jubilate* became almost a
diary, written one, two or three lines a day, a highly sophisticated
attempt by a learned man to preserve the astonishingly varied
materials of his knowledge. It was neither published nor intended to
be published in Smart's time. The *Jubilate* in both its form and its
content gives a misleading impression of the kind of poet Smart was,
falsely emphasizing peripheral aspects of his poetic experimentation,
and the mystical element in his knowledge. The recovery of the
manuscript, paradoxically, has drawn critical attention away from

the substantial body of later published poetry, where Smart's achievement is less ambiguous, and in which his main sources are the Bible and a more orthodox western literary tradition.

Since Browning's *Parleyings*, however, there has been no doubt of the stature of Smart's greatest work, *A Song to David*, a beautifully-made and rhetorically self-conscious high lyric of sustained devotion. Smart found in King David the perfect hero and 'the best poet which ever lived', incorporating all godly virtues and typifying the inspired poet-priest, the minister and now the recipient of praise:

> O THOU, that sit'st upon a throne,
> With harp of high majestic tone,
>   To praise the King of kings;
> And voice of heav'n-ascending swell,
> Which, while its deeper notes excell,
>   Clear, as a clarion, rings.
>
> To bless each valley, grove and coast,
> And charm the cherubs to the post
>   Of gratitude in throngs;
> To *keep* the days on Zion's mount,
> And send the year to his account,
>   With dances and with songs.

Stanzas 1, 2

In a long central passage (stanzas 51ff.) David is the great leader of the hymn of Adoration in which all nature joins, each creature, in a typically innocent Smart scenery, vividly and concisely imaged in pursuit of its characteristic activity, through the different seasons of the year:

> The laurels with the winter strive;
> The crocus burnishes alive
>   Upon the snow-clad earth:
> For ADORATION myrtles stay
> To keep the garden from dismay,
>   And bless the sight from dearth.
>
> The pheasant shows his pompous neck;
> And ermine, jealous of a speck,

> With fear eludes offence:
> The sable, with his glossy pride,
> For ADORATION is descried,
> Where frosts the wave condense.

Stanzas 61, 62

In such writing is to be seen Smart's mastery of stanzaic form, developed in his apprenticeship as a writer of popular verse for the magazines, and finding now its proper content. In the *Song* and *Hymns and Spiritual Songs* especially Smart perfected his technique of fitting within the stanza a religious vision both imaginative and precise. The few short lines, relatively simple in rhythm and rhyme-scheme, far from inhibiting complexity or subtlety of thought, provide an exact framework for compressed metaphor and pointed allusion. On a larger scale, the progression of the word ADORATION through the stanzas of this extended passage exemplifies the poem's use of schematic rhetoric, to be found too in the repetitive verbal organisation of the passage on David's virtues (stanzas 4-16), and most explicitly in the 'amplification in five degrees' with which the poem concludes. Here Smart finds in praise and prayer the super-lative of the sweet, the strong and the beauteous, the precious and the glorious, and in a triumphant climax brings together the salva-tion wrought by Christ, the faith of David the psalmist, and the accomplishment of his own psalm of praise, *exegi monumentum aere perennius*:

> Glorious—more glorious is the crown
> Of Him that brought salvation down
>   By meekness, call'd thy Son;
> Thou at stupendous truth believ'd,
> And now the matchless deed's atchiev'd,
>   DETERMINED, DARED, and DONE.

In the advertisement for the first edition printed in his *Poems on Several Occasions* (1763) Smart himself drew attention to the *Song*'s complicated coherence, 'the exact Regularity and Method with which it is conducted'. By this no doubt Smart intended the poem's numerical and thematic as well as its rhetorical ordering. He describes the *Song* in stanza 3 as 'the wreath I weave', using an image of cir-cular structure familiar to such earlier poets as Spenser, Donne and

Herbert. The stanzas are arranged in groups of three or seven, or multiples of these divine numbers, each group dealing with its own subject, as the prefatory list of contents explains. In a brilliant recent article Christopher M. Dennis has argued that the poem is organised symmetrically about a central group of twelve stanzas (38-49), where two frame-stanzas enclose ten which are 'an exercise upon the decalogue' and representative of the ten strings of David's instrument. So the construction of the poem invites us to see 'DAVID in the midst', singing his psalm of praise to the symbolic harp.

Presenting himself in *Jubilate Agno* as 'the Reviver of ADORATION amongst ENGLISH-MEN' (B2.332), and identifying himself in *A Song to David* with 'the great Author of The Book of Gratitude', Smart saw his role as the inventor of a new poetry of praise. The *Translation of the Psalms of David* and *Hymns and Spiritual Songs* were parts of a programme of liturgical and poetic reformation:

> But if the work be new,
> So shou'd the song be too.
>
> *Hymns* 9, stanza 5

Written in an established English tradition of versified and Christianized translations of the Psalms, Smart's version was 'Adapted to the Divine Service', and intended for music. Settings were composed especially for Smart's psalms by William Boyce and others, and separately published in the same year. Within the massive compass of this second tribute to David, Smart was able to experiment, with his usual technical facility, in a wide variety of metres. Less happily, Smart's method of expanding each verse of the Psalter into a stanza offered temptations to the mechanical and redundant which, despite his deep understanding of the Psalms, he did not everywhere escape.

More consistently impressive are the *Hymns and Spiritual Songs for the Fasts and Festivals of the Church of England*, a collection of devotional poems based firmly on the Bible and the prescriptions of the Prayer Book for each feast and fast day. They are, as Anglican hymns, unique in their period. The eighteenth century was a great age of hymn-writing by dissenters, Methodists and Evangelicals, but the Anglican church itself remained a psalm-singing body, and Smart was the only Anglican hymn-writer who was not a Methodist or Evangelical. His *Hymns* are distinct in both theology and style. Whereas the popular hymnody Calvinistically insists on the worthlessness of man's deeds and the corruptness of the world, Smart's *Hymns* show a typically Anglican respect for the essential goodness of man's heart and the value of good works, and present the creation as unfallen, a constant and cheerful reminder of God's goodness. In this Smart's poetry partakes of a more optimistic Anglican view of nature, of which Joseph Addison, in the *Spectator*, had been a spokesman: 'The Creation is a perpetual Feast to the Mind of a good Man, every thing he sees chears and delights him.' (*Spectator* 393, 31 May 1712.) Like the *Song*, the *Hymns* are in part a celebration of the gifts of the seasons, the evergreens of winter, the 'bell-flow'rs of the spring', the 'swelling fruits of summer', and a call to the creatures to bear a part in the chorus of thanksgiving:

> I speak for all—for them that fly,
> And for the race that swim;
> For all that dwell in moist and dry,
> Beasts, reptiles, flow'rs and gems to vie
> When gratitude begins her hymn.

Hymns 6, stanza 9

The popular hymns were meant to be sung by congregations which included the poor and simple, and they were intended to iterate the central tenets of Christian belief, or sectarian doctrine. Metaphor tended to be simple, biblical references straight, relatively unpoeticized quotation. By contrast, Smart's *Hymns* are sacred lyrics rather than congregational hymns. In language and figure they are highly sophisticated and poetic, related to an extensive tradition of religious verse which includes Herbert and Marvell as well as Milton, and finding in the Bible an abundance of themes and images, to be used imaginatively, transmuted to Smart's artistic purpose. The *Hymns* draw, as the *Song* does, upon seventeenth-century ideas of poetic organization. Smart calls his cycle a 'wreathed garland', and indeed the *Hymns* are a garland, the first line of each hymn picking up the last of its predecessor to make a circle, as Donne's sonnet sequence *La Corona* images its title in its structure. As in most of Smart's later published work, apparent difficulty in the *Hymns* derives less from the use of esoteric materials than from the extreme compression of his writing, the way in which briefest phrases fuse together

multiple significance and reference. The last seven lines of the
Circumcision hymn image a signet ring with a verbal 'device' around
its stone. This condensed metaphor has at least two, by no means
simply used, biblical sources, the signet of the Lord in Jeremiah
22.24, and God's seal of salvation from Revelations 7.2-4. Smart's
poetry follows a controlled, but often a figurative, logic. So, for
instance, part of the complex meaning of his Nativity hymn depends
on its setting of Christ's birth against a background of classical
pastoral, visible already in the 'swains of Solyma' of the second line,
and developed in the fourth stanza:

> If so young and thus eternal,
>   Michael tune the shepherd's reed,
> Where the scenes are ever vernal,
>   And the loves be love indeed!

In the lasting spring of this new Arcadia the Archangel Michael takes
over the reed of the shepherd-singer, and the pagan loves (cupids or
'amoretti') give way to Christ, who is love itself. A thematic parallel
is expressed with similar economy in stanza seven:

> Boreas now no longer winters
>   On the desolated coast;
> Oaks no more are riv'n in splinters
>   By the whirlwind and his host.

As the Saviour replaces the pagan divinity, so his New Testament of
Love supersedes the Old Testament dispensation of the angry God
who splintered the oaks of Bashan and came in the whirlwind.

Smart's second collection of hymns, the *Hymns for the Amusement
of Children* (1770), was intended, like the *Phaedrus* and *Parables*, for
an audience of children. These later hymns are both more obviously
conventional and less 'poetic' than the *Hymns and Spiritual Songs*,
with a special debt to the popular tradition of children's verse which
notably included John Bunyan's *Book for Boys and Girls* (1686),
Isaac Watts's *Divine Songs Attempted in Easy Language for the Use
of Children* (1715), and Charles Wesley's *Hymns for Children* (1763).
Smart's shares with these collections an avowedly pedagogical purpose,
'a plan,/To make good girls and boys' (*Hymns* 17, 'Praise', stanza 3).
The *Hymns for the Amusement of Children* are, in a way that perhaps
anticipates Blake's *Songs*, deliberately, and beautifully, simple:

> NOW's the time for mirth and play,
> Saturday's an holiday;
> Praise to heav'n unceasing yield,
> I've found a lark's nest in the field.
>
>   *Hymns* 33, 'For Saturday', stanza 1

Nonetheless in a number of hymns something of Smart's more mannered mature style, sinewed form and characteristic spiritual concerns survives:

> O highly rais'd above the ranks
> Of Angels—he cou'd e'en give thanks,
>   Self-rais'd and self-renew'd—
> Then who can praise, and love, and fear
> Enough?—since he himself, 'tis clear,
>   Is also gratitude.
>
>   *Hymns* 21, 'Generosity', stanza 4

> I'm the Phoenix of the singers,
>   That in upper Eden dwell;
> Hearing me Euphrates lingers,
>   As my wondrous tale I tell.
>
>   *Hymns* 22, 'Gratitude', stanza 6

In an important sense almost all the poetry Smart wrote after 1759 is religious poetry, its dominant theme 'Heav'nly gratitude'. 'On a Bed of Guernsey Lillies' (composed in 1763) once more celebrates the unceasing, and Christian, gifts of the seasons:

> 'Tis by succession of delight
>   That love supports his reign.

In *Hannah* (1764), the first of Smart's two oratorios, the miraculous fertility of Abraham's wife is seen as part of the grateful plenitude of nature. Smart's poems of secular compliment are also exercises on 'the grace of gratitude'. Smart makes gratitude the title and subject of his poem in memory of Thomas Seaton, who in founding the competition for poetry on the Attributes of the Supreme Being instituted an occasion for 'thanks & laud'. Gratitude to God is the motive both of the Seatonian poems and of David's Psalms, but there is another kind of necessary, and divine, gratitude, the memorialising praise of a mortal: 'Yet honour *Seaton*'s memory too.' By his references to Spenser's eulogy of Sidney (in his *Astrophel*), and Prior's of Dorset (in the Dedication of *Poems on Several Occasions*, 1709) Smart here makes clear that he was conscious of writing in a tradition, Renaissance, classical, and in his own view biblical, of poetry which presents examples of patriotic and religious virtue. *A Song to David* is partly of that tradition; 'Let us now praise famous men . . .', quotes Smart, from Ecclesiasticus 44, in his 1763 advertisement for the *Song*. In the ode to Admiral Pocock, the hero of the taking of Havannah in 1762, Smart gives poetic 'thanks to Heav'n' for the victory of a *'Christian* patriot', who combines valour and benevolence.

Second only to David as a poetic model for Smart was Horace. Smart's prose translation of Horace for Newbery, published in 1755, had been essentially hack-work. On his release from the madhouse he turned with evident enthusiasm to producing a verse translation, which combines an often playful wit with high seriousness. Horace was especially congenial to Smart as a poet of praise, whether addressing the godlike Augustus or the gods themselves. In his Preface Smart describes him as 'one of the most thankful men that ever lived' (p. xxx), and refers to the *Carmen Saeculare*, Horace's official celebratory song for the Saecular Games of 17 B.C., as 'the brightest monument of the *Heathen Psalmist* and *Roman worship*' (p. x). Horace was to Smart also a compelling example for a characteristically poetic language, a 'peculiarity of expression'. Partly this stemmed from 'the curiosity of choice diction', the revival of old words and the coining of new ones, or the use of old words in unfamiliar contexts:

> It is exceeding well
> To give a common word the *spell*,
> To greet you as intirely new.

> *Horace His Art of Poetry*

Besides this *curiosa felicitas* Smart also found in Horace, more generally: '. . . the beauty, force and vehemence of *Impression* . . . by which a Genius is impowered to throw an emphasis upon a word or sentence in such wise, that it cannot escape any reader of sheer good sense, and true critical sagacity' (p. xii). Smart has in mind the ways in which a poet makes his expression distinctive, and so forcibly communicates his meaning to the reader. The word 'impression' had been previously used by Smart, with these implications, in the *Jubilate*:

> For my talent is to give an impression upon words by punching,
>> that when the reader casts his eye upon 'em, he takes up the
>> image from the mould wch I have made.   B2.404

The modes of 'punching' certainly included for Smart 'peculiarity' of diction, concise and manifold metaphor, strenuous and unusual syntax. All these features may be found in Smart's verse translation of Horace, but they characterise also a great deal of the poetry Smart wrote after 1759. The following passages, in all of which may be found a clear though not a simple sense, typify the difficulties raised, and the rewards offered, by such a mode of writing:

> His furious foes no more malign'd
> As he such melody divin'd,
>> And sense and soul detain'd;
> Now striking strong, now soothing soft,
> He sent the godly sounds aloft,
>> Or in delight refrain'd.

A Song to David, stanza 28

> All creatures batten o'er their stores.

Ibid., stanza 63

> Sweet the musician's ardour beats,
> While his vague mind's in quest of sweets,
>> The choicest flow'rs to hive.

Ibid., stanza 73

> Way from guiltless natures winning.

Hymns and Spiritual Songs 1, stanza 4

> Ye that skill the flow'rs to fancy.

Ibid., 3, stanza 13

> Praise him ye cherubs of his breast,
>> The mercies of his love,
> Ere yet from guile and hate profest,
> The phenix makes his fragrant nest
>> In his own paradise above.

Ibid., 6, stanza 16

Why with such strength of thought devise,
    And aim at sublunary pelf,
Seek foreign realms?
                                    The Works of Horace, Ode 2.16

This pine, that o'er my villa tow'rs,
And from its eminence embow'rs,
    I dedicate alone to thee;
Where ev'ry year a pig shall bleed,
Lest his obliquity succeed
    Against thy fav'rite tree.
                                    Ibid., Ode 3.22

In the Preface to the verse Horace Impression, 'a talent or gift of Almighty God' (p. xii), is seen as not only a stylistic method and process, but dependent on matter and inspiration. Smart illustrates Impression by quotations from the Bible, Homer and Virgil, and insists: '. . . the force of *Impression* is always liveliest upon the eulogies of patriotism, gratitude, honour, and the like' (p. xiii). Smart is concerned not merely with style, but with the proper style for the poetry of praise, the patriotic eulogy of heroic and virtuous men, and the higher glorification of God. Impression is an aspect of sublime style, possible only in treating sublime subjects, and most eminent on the highest theme: '. . . we must confess this virtue to be far more powerful and abundant in the sacred writings . . .'; 'After all, . . . there is a littleness in the noblest poets among the Heathens when compared with the prodigious grandeur and genuine majesty of a *David* or *Isaiah*' (pp. xii, xvi).

As T. S. Eliot argued in his introductory essay (1930) to Samuel Johnson's *London* and *The Vanity of Human Wishes*, English poets between Pope and Wordsworth were faced with the problem of adapting inherited forms and language to a changing sensibility, of finding 'a style of writing for themselves, suited to the matter they wanted to talk about and the way in which they apprehended this matter'. So great a mind as Johnson could make the couplet of Dryden and Pope his own. Such lesser talents as Mark Akenside could not always avoid submergence in Miltonic blank verse. William Collins and Thomas Gray boldly and self-consciously returned to

Pindar's lyric model, and in their different ways attempted to give poetry what Gray called 'a language peculiar to itself' (*Correspondence*, p. 192). More consistently, perhaps more successfully, certainly with less influence than any of his contemporaries Smart made himself answerable for form and style. 'Sensibility alters from generation to generation in everybody, whether we will or no', Eliot reminds us; 'but expression is only altered by a man of genius.'

SELECT BOOKLIST

The Collected Poems of Christopher Smart. Ed. Norman Callan. 2 vols. London: Routledge, 1949. The most complete edition currently available.

Poems by Christopher Smart. Ed. Robert Brittain. Princeton: Princeton University Press, 1950. Extensive selection with superb Introduction and notes.

Rejoice in the Lamb. Ed. William Force Stead. London: Cape, 1939. The first printing of *Jubilate Agno*. Valuable notes.

Jubilate Agno. Ed. W. H. Bond. Cambridge: Harvard University Press, 1954. The standard edition.

A Song to David. Oxford: Clarendon Press, 1926. A type-facsimile of the first edition, 1763.

Hymns for the Amusement of Children. Oxford: Luttrell Society, 1947. A type-facsimile of the third edition, 1775, with fine Introduction by Edmund Blunden.

Hymns for the Amusement of Children. Menston: Scolar Press, 1973. Photographic facsimile of the Dublin edition of 1772.

G. J. Gray. 'A Bibliography of the Writings of Christopher Smart, with Biographical References.' *Transactions of the Bibliographical Society* 6 (1903), 268-303.

E. G. Ainsworth and C. E. Noyes. *Christopher Smart: a Biographical and Critical Study*. University of Missouri Studies 18, no. 4. Columbia, Missouri, 1943.

Donald Davie. 'Christopher Smart: Some Neglected Poems.' *Eighteenth-Century Studies* 3 (1969-70), 242-64. On the *Hymns and*

Spiritual Songs, Translation of the Psalms, verse Horace, and *Hymns for the Amusement of Children*.

Moira Dearnley. *The Poetry of Christopher Smart*. London: Routledge, 1969.

Christopher M. Dennis. 'A Structural Conceit in Smart's *Song to David*.' *Review of English Studies* NS 29 (1978), 257-66.

Raymond D. Havens. 'The Structure of Smart's *Song to David*.' *Review of English Studies* 14 (1938), 178-82.

William M. Merchant. 'Patterns of Reference in Smart's *Jubilate Agno*.' *Harvard Library Bulletin* 14 (1960), 20-26.

Arthur Sherbo. *Christopher Smart: Scholar of the University*. East Lansing: Michigan State University Press, 1967. The standard biography.

Patricia M. Spacks. *The Poetry of Vision: Five Eighteenth-Century Poets*. Cambridge: Harvard University Press, 1967.

Jean Wilkinson. 'Three Sets of Religious Poems.' *Huntington Library Quarterly* 36 (1973), 203-26. On Herbert's *The Temple*, Smart's *Hymns and Spiritual Songs* and Keble's *Christian Year*.

Karina Williamson. 'Christopher Smart's *Hymns and Spiritual Songs*.' *Philological Quarterly* 38 (1959), 413-24.

ON THE GOODNESS OF THE SUPREME BEING
A Poetical Essay
The 1755 Seatonian Prize Poem. First edition Cambridge, 1756 [text].

ORPHEUS, for *so the Gentiles call'd thy name,
Israel's sweet Psalmist, who alone couldst wake
Th'inanimate to motion; who alone
The joyful hillocks, the applauding rocks,
And floods with musical persuasion drew;
Thou who to hail and snow gav'st voice and sound,
And mad'st the mute melodious!—greater yet
Was thy divinest skill, and rul'd o'er more
Than art and nature; for thy tuneful touch
Drove trembling Satan from the heart of Saul,
And quell'd the evil Angel:—in this breast
Some portion of thy genuine spirit breathe,
And lift me from myself, each thought impure
Banish; each low idea raise, refine,
Enlarge and sanctify;—so shall the muse
Above the stars aspire, and aim to praise
Her God on earth, as he is prais'd in heaven.
    Immense Creator! whose all-pow'rful hand
Fram'd universal Being, and whose Eye
Saw like thyself, that all things form'd were good;
Where shall the tim'rous bard thy praise begin,
Where end the purest sacrifice of song,
And just thanksgiving?—The thought-kindling light,
Thy prime production, darts upon my mind
Its vivifying beams, my heart illumines,
And fills my soul with gratitude and Thee.
Hail to the chearful rays of ruddy morn,
That paint the streaky East, and blithsome rouse
The birds, the cattle, and mankind from rest!
Hail to the freshness of the early breeze,
And Iris dancing on the new-fall'n dew!

*See this conjecture strongly supported by *Delany*, in his *Life of David*. [Smart]

Without the aid of yonder golden globe
Lost were the garnet's lustre, lost the lilly,
The tulip and auricula's spotted pride;
Lost were the peacock's plumage, to the sight
So pleasing in its pomp and glossy glow.
O thrice-illustrious! were it not for thee
Those pansies, that reclining from the bank,
View thro' th'immaculate, pellucid stream
Their portraiture in the inverted heaven,
Might as well change their triple boast, the white,
The purple, and the gold, that far outvie
The Eastern monarch's garb, ev'n with the dock,
Ev'n with the baneful hemlock's irksome green.
Without thy aid, without thy gladsome beams
The tribes of woodland warblers wou'd remain
Mute on the bending branches, nor recite
The praise of him, who, e'er he form'd their lord,
Their voices tun'd to transport, wing'd their flight,
And bade them call for nurture, and receive;
And lo! they call; the blackbird and the thrush,
The woodlark, and the redbreast jointly call;
He hears and feeds their feather'd families,
He feeds his sweet musicians,—nor neglects
Th'invoking ravens in the greenwood wide;
And tho' their throats coarse ruttling hurt the ear,
They mean it all for music, thanks and praise
They mean, and leave ingratitude to man,—
But not to all,—for hark the organs blow
Their swelling notes round the cathedral's dome,
And grace th'harmonious choir, celestial feast
To pious ears, and med'cine of the mind;
The thrilling trebles and the manly base
Join in accordance meet, and with one voice
All to the sacred subject suit their song.
While in each breast sweet melancholy reigns
Angelically pensive, till the joy
Improves and purifies;—the solemn scene

The Sun thro' storied panes surveys with awe,
And bashfully with-holds each bolder beam.
Here, as her home, from morn to eve frequents
The cherub Gratitude;—behold her Eyes!
With love and gladness weepingly they shed
Extatic smiles; the incense, that her hands
Uprear, is sweeter than the breath of May
Caught from the nectarine's blossom, and her voice
Is more than voice can tell; to him she sings,
To him who feeds, who clothes and who adorns,
Who made and who preserves, whatever dwells
In air, in stedfast earth or fickle sea.
O He is good, he is immensely good!
Who all things form'd and form'd them all for man;
Who mark'd the climates, varied every zone,
Dispensing all his blessings for the best
In order and in beauty:—rise, attend,
Attest, and praise, ye quarters of the world!
Bow down, ye elephants, submissive bow
To him, who made the mite; tho'Asia's pride,
Ye carry armies on your tow'r-crown'd backs,
And grace the turban'd tyrants, bow to him
Who is as great, as perfect and as good
In his less-striking wonders, till at length
The eye's at fault and seeks th'assisting glass.
Approach and bring from Araby the blest
The fragrant cassia, frankincense and myrrh,
And meekly kneeling at the altar's foot
Lay all the tributary incense down.
Stoop, sable Africa, with rev'rence stoop,
And from thy brow take off the painted plume;
With golden ingots all thy camels load
T'adorn his temples, hasten with thy spear
Reverted, and thy trusty bow unstrung,
While unpursu'd thy lions roam and roar,
And ruin'd tow'rs, rude rocks and caverns wide
Remurmur to the glorious, surly sound.

And thou, fair Indian, whose immense domain
To counterpoise the Hemisphere extends,
Haste from the West, and with thy fruits and flow'rs,
Thy mines and med'cines, wealthy maid, attend.
More than the plenteousness so fam'd to flow
By fabling bards from Amalthea's horn
Is thine; thine therefore be a portion due
Of thanks and praise: come with thy brilliant crown
And vest of furr; and from thy fragrant lap
Pomegranates and the rich *ananas pour.
But chiefly thou, Europa, seat of grace
And Christian excellence, his goodness own,
Forth from ten thousand temples pour his praise;
Clad in the armour of the living God
Approach, unsheath the spirit's flaming sword;
Faith's shield, Salvation's glory,—compass'd helm
With fortitude assume, and o'er your heart
Fair truth's invulnerable breast-plate spread;
Then join the general chorus of all worlds,
And let the song of charity begin
In strains seraphic, and melodious pray'r.
'O all-sufficient, all-beneficent,
Thou God of Goodness and of glory, hear!
Thou, who to lowliest minds dost condescend,
Assuming passions to enforce thy laws,
Adopting jealousy to prove thy love:
Thou, who resign'd humility uphold,
Ev'n as the florist props the drooping rose,
But quell tyrannic pride with peerless pow'r,
Ev'n as the tempest rives the stubborn oak:
O all-sufficient, all beneficent,
Thou God of goodness and of glory hear!
Bless all mankind, and bring them in the end
To heav'n, to immortality, and THEE!'

---

*Ananas the Indian name for Pine-Apples. [Smart]

JUBILATE AGNO

Written 1759-63. First published as *Rejoice in the Lamb*, ed. W. F. Stead, 1939.

Fragment A

Lines 1-9

1.   REJOICE in God, O ye Tongues; give the glory to the Lord, and the Lamb.

Nations, and languages, and every Creature, in which is the breath of Life.

Let man and beast appear before him, and magnify his name together.

Let Noah and his company approach the throne of Grace, and do homage to the Ark of their Salvation.

5.   Let Abraham present a Ram, and worship the God of his Redemption.

Let Isaac, the Bridegroom, kneel with his Camels, and bless the hope of his pilgrimage.

Let Jacob, and his speckled Drove adore the good Shepherd of Israel.

Let Esau offer a scape Goat for his seed, and rejoice in the blessing of God his father.

Let Nimrod, the mighty hunter, bind a Leopard to the altar, and consecrate his spear to the Lord.

Lines 20-57

20.   Let Merari praise the wisdom and power of God with the Coney, who scoopeth the rock, and archeth in the sand.

Let Kohath serve with the Sable, and bless God in the ornaments of the Temple.

Let Jehoiada bless God with an Hare, whose mazes are determined for the health of the body and to parry the adversary.

Let Ahitub humble himself with an Ape before Almighty God, who is the maker of variety and pleasantry.

Let Abiathar with a fox praise the name of the Lord, who ballances craft against strength and skill against number.

25.   Let Moses, the Man of God, bless with a Lizard, in the sweet majesty of good-nature, and the magnanimity of meekness.

Let Joshua praise God with an Unicorn—the swiftness of the Lord, and the strength of the Lord, and the spear of the Lord mighty in battle.

Let Caleb with an Ounce praise the Lord of the Land of beauty and rejoice in the blessing of his good Report.

Let Othniel praise God with the Rhinoceros, who put on his armour for the reward of beauty in the Lord.

Let Tola bless with the Toad, which is the good creature of God, tho' his virtue is in the secret, and his mention is not made.

30.   Let Barak praise with the Pard—and great is the might of the faithful and great is the Lord in the nail of Jael and the sword of the Son of Abinoam.

Let Gideon bless with the Panther—the Word of the Lord is invincible by him that lappeth from the brook.

Let Jotham praise with the Urchin, who took up his parable and provided himself for the adversary to kick against the pricks.

Let Boaz, the Builder of Judah, bless with the Rat, which dwelleth in hardship and peril, that they may look to themselves and keep their houses in order.

Let Obed-Edom with a Dormouse praise the Name of the Lord God his Guest for increase of his store and for peace.

35.   Let Abishai bless with the Hyæna—the terror of the Lord, and the fierceness of his wrath against the foes of the King and of Israel.

Let Ethan praise with the Flea, his coat of mail, his piercer, and his vigour, which wisdom and providence have contrived to attract observation and to escape it.

Let Heman bless with the Spider, his warp and his woof, his subtlety and industry, which are good.

Let Chalcol praise with the Beetle, whose life is precious in the sight of God, tho' his appearance is against him.

Let Darda with a Leech bless the Name of the Physician of body & soul.

40.   Let Mahol praise the Maker of Earth and Sea with the Otter, whom God has given to dive and to burrow for his preservation.

       Let David bless with the Bear—The beginning of victory to the Lord—to the Lord the perfection of excellence—Hallelujah from the heart of God, and from the hand of the artist inimitable, and from the echo of the heavenly harp in sweetness magnifical and mighty.

       Let Solomon praise with the Ant, and give the glory to the Fountain of all Wisdom.

       Let Romamti-Ezer bless with the Ferret—the Lord is a rewarder of them, that diligently seek him.

       Let Samuel, the Minister from a child, without ceasing praise with the Porcupine, which is the creature of defence and stands upon his arms continually.

45.   Let Nathan and the Badger bless God for his retired fame, and privacy inaccessible to slander.

       Let Joseph, who from the abundance of his blessing may spare to him that lacketh, praise with the Crocodile, which is pleasant and pure, when he is interpreted, tho' his look is of terror and offence.

       Let Esdras bless Christ Jesus with the Rose and his people, which is a nation of living sweetness.

       Let Mephibosheth with the Cricket praise the God of chearfulness, hospitality, and gratitude.

       Let Shallum with the Frog bless God for the meadows of Canaan, the fleece, the milk and the honey.

50.   Let Hilkiah praise with the Weasel, which sneaks for his prey in craft, and dwelleth at ambush.

       Let Job bless with the Worm—the life of the Lord is in Humiliation, the Spirit also and the truth.

       Let Elihu bless with the Tortoise, which is food for praise and thanksgiving.

       Let Hezekiah praise with the Dromedary—the zeal for the glory of God is excellence, and to bear his burden is grace.

       Let Zadoc worship with the Mole—before honour is humility, and he that looketh low shall learn.

55.   Let Gad with the Adder bless in the simplicity of the preacher
and the wisdom of the creature.

Let Tobias bless Charity with his Dog, who is faithful, vigilant,
and a friend in poverty.

Let Anna bless God with the Cat, who is worthy to be presented
before the throne of grace, when he has trampled upon the
idol in his prank.

Fragment B1, 'Let' and 'For' lines

Lines 1-30

1.   Let Elizur rejoice with the Partridge, who is a prisoner of state
and is proud of his keepers.

Let Shedeur rejoice with Pyrausta, who dwelleth in a medium
of fire, which God hath adapted for him.

Let Shelumiel rejoice with Olor, who is of a goodly savour,
and the very look of him harmonizes the mind.

Let Jael rejoice with the Plover, who whistles for his live,
and foils the marksmen and their guns.

5.   Let Raguel rejoice with the Cock of Portugal—God send good
Angels to the allies of England!

Let Hobab rejoice with Necydalus, who is the Greek of a
Grub.

Let Zurishaddai with the Polish Cock rejoice—the Lord restore
peace to Europe.

Let Zuar rejoice with the Guinea Hen—the Lord add to his
mercies in the WEST!

Let Chesed rejoice with Strepsiceros, whose weapons are the
ornaments of his peace.

10.   Let Hagar rejoice with Gnesion, who is the right sort of eagle,
and towers the highest.

Let Libni rejoice with the Redshank, who migrates not but is
translated to the upper regions.

Let Nahshon rejoice with the Seabreese, the Lord give the
sailors of his Spirit.

Let Helon rejoice with the Woodpecker—the Lord encourage
the propagation of trees!

1.   For I am not without authority in my jeopardy, which I derive
       inevitably from the glory of the name of the Lord.

       For I bless God whose name is Jealous—and there is a zeal to
       deliver us from everlasting burnings.

       For my existimation is good even amongst the slanderers and
       my memory shall arise for a sweet savour unto the Lord.

       For I bless the PRINCE of PEACE and pray that all the guns
       may be nail'd up, save such as are for the rejoicing days.

5.   For I have abstained from the blood of the grape and that even
       at the Lord's table.

       For I have glorified God in GREEK and LATIN, the consec-
       rated languages spoken by the Lord on earth.

       For I meditate the peace of Europe amongst family bickerings
       and domestic jars.

       For the HOST is in the WEST—the Lord make us thankful
       unto salvation.

       For I preach the very GOSPEL of CHRIST without comment
       & with this weapon shall I slay envy.

10.   For I bless God in the rising generation, which is on my side.

       For I have translated in the charity, which makes things better
       & I shall be translated myself at the last.

       For he that walked upon the sea, hath prepared the floods
       with the Gospel of peace.

       For the merciful man is merciful to his beast, and to the trees
       that give them shelter.

Let Amos rejoice with the Coote—prepare to meet thy God,
O Israel.

15. Let Ephah rejoice with Buprestis, the Lord endue us with
temperance & humanity, till every cow have her mate!

Let Sarah rejoice with the Redwing, whose harvest is in the
frost and snow.

Let Rebekah rejoice with Iynx, who holds his head on one side
to deceive the adversary.

Let Shuah rejoice with Boa, which is the vocal serpent.

Let Ehud rejoice with Onocrotalus, whose braying is for the
glory of God, because he makes the best music in his power.

20. Let Shamgar rejoice with Otis, who looks about him for the
glory of God, & sees the horizon compleat at once.

Let Bohan rejoice with the Scythian Stag—he is beef and
breeches against want & nakedness.

Let Achsah rejoice with the Pigeon who is an antidote to
malignity and will carry a letter.

Let Tohu rejoice with the Grouse—the Lord further the
cultivating of heaths & the peopling of deserts.

Let Hillel rejoice with Ammodytes, whose colour is deceitful
and he plots against the pilgrim's feet.

25. Let Eli rejoice with Leucon—he is an honest fellow, which is a
rarity.

Let Jemuel rejoice with Charadrius, who is from the HEIGHT
& the sight of him is good for the jaundice.

Let Pharoah rejoice with Anataria, whom God permits to prey
upon the ducks to check their increase.

Let Lotan rejoice with Sauterelle. Blessed be the name of the
Lord from the Lote-tree to the Palm.

Let Dishon rejoice with the Landrail, God give his grace to
the society for preserving the game.

30. Let Hushim rejoice with the King's Fisher, who is of royal
beauty, tho' plebeian size.

For he hath turned the shadow of death into the morning, the
    Lord is his name.

15.   For I am come home again, but there is nobody to kill the calf
    or to pay the musick.

For the hour of my felicity, like the womb of Sarah, shall
    come at the latter end.

For I shou'd have avail'd myself of waggery, had not malice
    been multitudinous.

For there are still serpents that can speak—God bless my head,
    my heart & my heel.

For I bless God that I am of the same seed as Ehud, Mutius
    Scævola, and Colonel Draper.

20.   For the word of God is a sword on my side—no matter what
    other weapon a stick or a straw.

For I have adventured myself in the name of the Lord, and he
    hath mark'd me for his own.

For I bless God for the Postmaster general & all conveyancers
    of letters under his care especially Allen & Shelvock.

For my grounds in New Canaan shall infinitely compensate for
    the flats & maynes of Staindrop Moor.

For the praise of God can give to a mute fish the notes of a
    nightingale.

25.   For I have seen the White Raven & Thomas Hall of Willingham
    & am myself a greater curiosity than both.

For I look up to heaven which is my prospect to escape envy
    by surmounting it.

For if Pharoah had known Joseph, he would have blessed God
    & me for the illumination of the people.

For I pray God to bless improvements in gardening till London
    be a city of palm-trees.

For I pray to give his grace to the poor of England, that
    Charity be not offended & that benevolence may increase.

30.   For in my nature I quested for beauty, but God, God hath
    sent me to sea for pearls.

Lines 45-60

45. Let Areli rejoice with the Criel, who is a dwarf that towereth above others.

Let Phuvah rejoice with Platycerotes, whose weapons of defence keep them innocent.

Let Shimron rejoice with the Kite, who is of more value than many sparrows.

Let Sered rejoice with the Wittal—a silly bird is wise unto his own preservation.

Let Elon rejoice with Attelabus, who is the Locust without wings.

50. Let Jahleel rejoice with the Woodcock, who liveth upon suction and is pure from his diet.

Let Shuni rejoice with the Gull, who is happy in not being good for food.

Let Ezbon rejoice with Musimon, who is from the ram and she-goat.

Let Barkos rejoice with the Black Eagle, which is the least of his species and the best-natured.

Let Bedan rejoice with Ossifrage—the bird of prey and the man of prayer.

55. Let Naomi rejoice with Pseudosphece, who is between a wasp and a hornet.

Let Ruth rejoice with the Tumbler—it is a pleasant thing to feed him and be thankful.

Let Ram rejoice with the Fieldfare, who is a good gift from God in the season of scarcity.

Let Manoah rejoice with Cerastes, who is a Dragon with horns.

Let Talmai rejoice with Alcedo, who makes a cradle for its young, which is rock'd by the winds.

60. Let Bukki rejoice with the Buzzard, who is clever, with the reputation of a silly fellow.

45.   For I am a little fellow, which is entitled to the great mess by the benevolence of God my father.

For I this day made over my inheritance to my mother in consideration of her infirmities.

For I this day made over my inheritance to my mother in consideration of her age.

For I this day made over my inheritance to my mother in consideration of her poverty.

For I bless the thirteenth of August, in which I had the grace to obey the voice of Christ in my conscience.

50.   For I bless the thirteenth of August, in which I was willing to run all hazards for the sake of the name of the Lord.

For I bless the thirteenth of August, in which I was willing to be called a fool for the sake of Christ.

For I lent my flocks and my herds and my lands at once unto the Lord.

For nature is more various than observation tho' observers be innumerable.

For Agricola is Γεωργος.

55.   For I pray God to bless POLLY in the blessing of Naomi and assign her to the house of David.

For I am in charity with the French who are my foes and Moabites because of the Moabitish woman.

For my Angel is always ready at a pinch to help me out and to keep me up.

For CHRISTOPHER must slay the Dragon with a PHEON's head.

For they have seperated me and my bosom, whereas the right comes by setting us together.

60.   For Silly fellow! Silly fellow! is against me and belongeth neither to me nor my family.

Lines 123-132

LET PETER rejoice with the MOON FISH who keeps up the
   life in the waters by night.

Let Andrew rejoice with the Whale, who is arrayd in beauteous
   blue & is a combination of bulk & activity.

125. Let James rejoice with the Skuttle-Fish, who foils his foe by
   the effusion of his ink.

Let John rejoice with Nautilus who spreads his sail & plies his
   oar, and the Lord is his pilot.

Let Philip rejoice with Boca, which is the fish that can speak.

Let Bartholomew rejoice with the Eel, who is pure in propor-
   tion to where he is found & how he is used.

Let Thomas rejoice with the Sword-Fish, whose aim is perpetual
   & strength insuperable.

130. Let Matthew rejoice with Uranoscopus, whose eyes are lifted
   up to God.

Let James the less, rejoice with the Haddock, who brought
   the piece of money for the Lord and Peter.

Let Jude bless with the Bream, who is of melancholy from his
   depth and serenity.

FOR I pray the Lord JESUS that cured the LUNATICK to be
merciful to all my brethren and sisters in these houses.

For they work me with their harping-irons, which is a barbarous
instrument, because I am more unguarded than others.

125. For the blessing of God hath been on my epistles, which I have
written for the benefit of others.

For I bless God that the CHURCH OF ENGLAND is one of
the SEVEN ev'n the candlestick of the Lord.

For the ENGLISH TONGUE shall be the language of the
WEST.

For I pray Almighty CHRIST to bless the MAGDALEN
HOUSE & to forward a National purification.

For I have the blessing of God in the three POINTS of man-
hood, of the pen, of the sword, & of chivalry.

130. For I am inquisitive in the Lord, and defend the philosophy
of the scripture against vain deceit.

For the nets come down from the eyes of the Lord to fish
up men to their salvation.

For I have a greater compass both of mirth and melancholy
than another.

Fragment B1, 'For' lines

Lines 224-252

For the AIR is purified by prayer which is made aloud and with all our might.

225. For loud prayer is good for weak lungs and for a vitiated throat.

For SOUND is propagated in the spirit and in all directions.

For the VOICE of a figure is compleat in all its parts.

For a man speaks HIMSELF from the crown of his head to the sole of his feet.

For a LION roars HIMSELF compleat from head to tail.

230. For all these things are seen in the spirit which makes the beauty of prayer.

For all whispers and unmusical sounds in general are of the Adversary.

For 'I will hiss saith the Lord' is God's denunciation of death.

For applause or the clapping of the hands is the natural action of a man on the descent of the glory of God.

For EARTH which is an intelligence hath a voice and a propensity to speak in all her parts.

235. For ECHO is the soul of the voice exerting itself in hollow places.

For ECHO cannot act but when she can parry the adversary.

For ECHO is greatest in Churches and where she can assist in prayer.

For a good voice hath its Echo with it and it is attainable by much supplication.

For the VOICE is from the body and the spirit—and is a body and a spirit.

240. For the prayers of good men are therefore visible to second-sighted persons.

For HARPSICHORDS are best strung with gold wire.

For HARPS and VIOLS are best strung with Indian weed.

For the GERMAN FLUTE is an indirect—the common flute good, bless the Lord Jesus BENJAMIN HALLET.

For the feast of TRUMPETS should be kept up, that being the most direct & acceptable of all instruments.

245. For the TRUMPET of God is a blessed intelligence & so are all
the instruments in HEAVEN.

For GOD the father Almighty plays upon the HARP of
stupendous magnitude and melody.

For innumerable Angels fly out at every touch and his tune is
a work of creation.

For at that time malignity ceases and the devils themselves are
at peace.

For this time is perceptible to man by a remarkable stillness
and serenity of soul.

250. For the Æolian harp is improveable into regularity.

For when it is so improved it will be known to be the SHAWM.

For it woud be better if the LITURGY were musically per-
formed.

Fragment B2

Lines 305-340

305. For before the NATIVITY is the dead of the winter and after
it the quick.

For the sin against the HOLY GHOST is INGRATITUDE.

For stuff'd guts make no music; strain them strong and you
shall have sweet melody.

For the SHADOW is of death, which is the Devil, who can
make false and faint images of the works of Almighty God.

For every man beareth death about him ever since the trans-
gression of Adam, but in perfect light there is no shadow.

310. For all Wrath is Fire, which the adversary blows upon and
exasperates.

For SHADOW is a fair Word from God, which is not return-
able till the furnace comes up.

For the ECLIPSE is of the adversary—blessed be the name of
Jesus for Whisson of Trinity.

For the shadow is his and the penumbra is his and his the per-
plexity of the phenomenon.

For the eclipses happen at times when the light is defective.

315. For the more the light is defective, the more the powers of
     darkness prevail.
     For deficiencies happen by the luminaries crossing one another.
     For the SUN is an intelligence and an angel of the human form.
     For the MOON is an intelligence and an angel in shape like a
     woman.
     For they are together in the spirit every night like man and wife.
320. For Justice is infinitely beneath Mercy in nature and office.
     For the Devil himself may be just in accusation and punishment.
     For HELL is without eternity from the presence of Almighty
     God.
     For Volcanos & burning mountains are where the adversary
     hath most power.
     For the angel GRATITUDE is my wife—God bring me to her
     or her to me.
325. For the propagation of light is quick as the divine Conception.
     For FROST is damp & unwholesome air candied to fall to the
     best advantage.
     For I am the Lord's News-Writer—the scribe-evangelist—
     Widow Mitchel, Gun & Grange bless the Lord Jesus.
     For Adversity above all other is to be deserted of the grace of
     God.
     For in the divine Idea this Eternity is compleat & the Word is a
     making many more.
330. For there is a forlorn hope ev'n for impenitent sinners because
     the furnace itself must be the crown of Eternity.
     For my hope is beyond Eternity in the bosom of God my
     saviour.
     For by the grace of God I am the Reviver of ADORATION
     amongst ENGLISH-MEN.
     For being desert-ed is to have desert in the sight of God and
     intitles one to the Lord's merit.
     For things that are not in the sight of men are thro' God of
     infinite concern.
335. For envious men have exceeding subtlety quippe qui in—videant.
     For avaricious men are exceeding subtle like the soul seperated
     from the body.

For their attention is on a sinking object which perishes.

For they can go beyond the children of light in matters of
their own misery.

For Snow is the dew candied and cherishes.

340. For TIMES and SEASONS are the Lord's—Man is no
CHRONOLOGER.

Lines 492-510

For the doubling of flowers is the improvement of the gardners
talent.

For the flowers are great blessings.

For the Lord made a Nosegay in the medow with his disciples
& preached upon the lily.

495. For the angels of God took it out of his hand and carried it to
the Height.

For a man cannot have publick spirit, who is void of private
benevolence.

For there is no Height in which there are not flowers.

For flowers have great virtues for all the senses.

For the flower glorifies God and the root parries the adversary.

500. For the flowers have their angels even the words of God's
Creation.

For the warp & woof of flowers are worked by perpetual
moving spirits.

For flowers are good both for the living and the dead.

For there is a language of flowers.

For there is a sound reasoning upon all flowers.

505. For elegant phrases are nothing but flowers.

For flowers are peculiarly the poetry of Christ.

For flowers are medicinal.

For flowers are musical in ocular harmony.

For the right names of flowers are yet in heaven. God make
gardners better nomenclators.

510. For the Poorman's nosegay is an introduction to a Prince.

Lines 584-599

For the spiritual musick is as follows.
585. For there is the thunder-stop, which is the voice of God direct.
For the rest of the stops are by their rhimes.
For the trumpet rhimes are sound bound, soar more and the like.
For the Shawm rhimes are lawn fawn moon boon and the like.
For the harp rhimes are sing ring, string & the like.
590. For the cymbal rhimes are bell well toll soul & the like.
For the flute rhimes are tooth youth suit mute & the like.
For the dulcimer rhimes are grace place beat heat & the like.
For the Clarinet rhimes are clean seen and the like.
For the Bassoon rhimes are pass, class and the like. God be
gracious to Baumgarden.
595. For the dulcimer are rather van fan & the like and grace place
&c are of the bassoon.
For beat heat, weep peep &c are of the pipe.
For every word has its marrow in the English tongue for order
and for delight.
For the dissyllables such as able, table &c are the fiddle rhimes.
For all dissyllables and some trissyllables are fiddle rhimes.

Lines 626-643

For languages work into one another by their bearings.
For the power of some animal is predominant in every language.
For the power and spirit of a CAT is in the Greek.
For the sound of a cat is in the most useful preposition
κατ᾽ ευχην.
630. For the pleasantry of a cat at pranks is in the language ten
thousand times over.
For JACK UPON PRANCK is in the performance of περι
together or seperate.
For Clapperclaw is in the grappling of the words upon one
another in all the modes of versification.
For the sleekness of a cat is in his αγλαιηφι.
For the Greek is thrown from heaven and falls upon its feet.
635. For the Greek when distracted from the lines is sooner restored
to rank & rallied into some form than any other.

For the purring of a Cat is his Τρυζει.

For his cry is ουαι which I am sorry for.

For the Mouse (Mus) prevails in Latin.

For edi-mus, bibi-mus, vivi-mus—ore-mus.

640   For the Mouse is a creature of great personal valour.

For—this is a true case—Cat takes female mouse from the company of male—male mouse will not depart, but stands threatning & daring.

For this is as much as to challenge, if you will let her go, I will engage you, as prodigious a creature as you are.

For the Mouse is of an hospitable disposition.

Lines 697-770

For I will consider my Cat Jeoffry.

For he is the servant of the Living God duly and daily serving him.

For at the first glance of the glory of God in the East he worships in his way.

700.   For is this done by wreathing his body seven times round with elegant quickness.

For then he leaps up to catch the musk, wch is the blessing of God upon his prayer.

For he rolls upon prank to work it in.

For having done duty and received blessing he begins to consider himself.

For this he performs in ten degrees.

705.   For first he looks upon his fore-paws to see if they are clean.

For secondly he kicks up behind to clear away there.

For thirdly he works it upon stretch with the fore paws extended.

For fourthly he sharpens his paws by wood.

For fifthly he washes himself.

710.   For Sixthly he rolls upon wash.

For Seventhly he fleas himself, that he may not be interrupted upon the beat.

For Eighthly he rubs himself against a post.

For Ninthly he looks up for his instructions.

For Tenthly he goes in quest of food.

715. For having consider'd God and himself he will consider his
neighbour.

For if he meets another cat he will kiss her in kindness.

For when he takes his prey he plays with it to give it a chance.

For one mouse in seven escapes by his dallying.

For when his day's work is done his business more properly
begins.

720. For he keeps the Lord's watch in the night against the adversary.

For he counteracts the powers of darkness by his electrical
skin & glaring eyes.

For he counteracts the Devil, who is death, by brisking about
the life.

For in his morning orisons he loves the sun and the sun loves
him.

For he is of the tribe of Tiger.

725. For the Cherub Cat is a term of the Angel Tiger.

For he has the subtlety and hissing of a serpent, which in
goodness he suppresses.

For he will not do destruction if he is well-fed, neither will he
spit without provocation.

For he purrs in thankfulness, when God tells him he's a good
Cat.

For he is an instrument for the children to learn benevolence
upon.

730. For every house is incompleat without him & a blessing is
lacking in the spirit.

For the Lord commanded Moses concerning the cats at the
departure of the Children of Israel from Egypt.

For every family had one cat at least in the bag.

For the English Cats are the best in Europe.

For he is the cleanest in the use of his fore-paws of any
quadrupede.

735. For the dexterity of his defence is an instance of the love of
God to him exceedingly.

For he is the quickest to his mark of any creature.

For he is tenacious of his point.

For he is a mixture of gravity and waggery.

For he knows that God is his Saviour.

740. For there is nothing sweeter than his peace when at rest.

For there is nothing brisker than his life when in motion.

For he is of the Lord's poor and so indeed is he called by benevolence perpetually—Poor Jeoffry! poor Jeoffry! the rat has bit thy throat.

For I bless the name of the Lord Jesus that Jeoffry is better.

For the divine spirit comes about his body to sustain it in compleat cat.

745. For his tongue is exceeding pure so that it has in purity what it wants in musick.

For he is docile and can learn certain things.

For he can set up with gravity which is patience upon approbation.

For he can fetch and carry, which is patience in employment.

For he can jump over a stick which is patience upon proof positive.

750. For he can spraggle upon waggle at the word of command.

For he can jump from an eminence into his master's bosom.

For he can catch the cork and toss it again.

For he is hated by the hypocrite and miser.

For the former is afraid of detection.

755. For the latter refuses the charge.

For he camels his back to bear the first notion of business.

For he is good to think on, if a man would express himself neatly.

For he made a great figure in Egypt for his signal services.

For he killed the Icneumon-rat very pernicious by land.

760. For his ears are so acute that they sting again.

For from this proceeds the passing quickness of his attention.

For by stroaking of him I have found out electricity.

For I have perceived God's light about him both wax and fire.

For the Electrical fire is the spiritual substance, which God sends from heaven to sustain the bodies both of man and beast.

765. For God has blessed him in the variety of his movements.

For, tho he cannot fly, he is an excellent clamberer.

For his motions upon the face of the earth are more than any
    other quadrupede.

For he can tread to all the measures upon the musick.

For he can swim for life.

770. For he can creep.

Fragment C

Lines 1-33

For H is a spirit and therefore he is God.

For I is person and therefore he is God.

For K is king and therefore he is God.

For L is love and therefore he is God.

5. For M is musick and therefore he is God.

For N is novelty and therefore he is God.

For O is over and therefore he is God.

For P is power and therefore he is God.

For Q is quick and therefore he is God.

10. For R is right and therefore he is God.

For S is soul and therefore he is God.

For T is truth and therefore he is God.

For U is union and therefore he is God.

For W is worth and therefore he is God.

15. For X has the pow'r of three and therefore he is God.

For Y is yea and therefore he is God.

For Z is zeal and therefore he is God, whom I pray to be
    gracious to the Widow Davis and Davis the Bookseller.

For Christ being A and Ω is all the intermediate letters without
    doubt.

For there is a mystery in numbers.

20. For One is perfect and good being at unity in himself.

For Two is the most imperfect of all numbers.

For every thing infinitely perfect is Three.

For the Devil is two being without God.

For he is an evil spirit male and female.

25. For he is called the Duce by foolish invocation on that account.

For Three is the simplest and best of all numbers.

For Four is good being square.

For Five is not so good in itself but works well in combination.

For Five is not so good in itself as it consists of two and three.

30.   For Six is very good consisting of twice three.

For Seven is very good consisting of two compleat numbers.

For Eight is good for the same reason and propitious to me
     Eighth of March 1761 hallelujah.

For Nine is a number very good and harmonious.

Lines 52-64

For the story of Orpheus is of the truth.

For there was such a person a cunning player on the harp.

For he was a believer in the true God and assisted in the spirit.

55.   For he playd upon the harp in the spirit by breathing upon
     the strings.

For this will affect every thing that is sustained by the spirit
     even every thing in nature.

For it is the business of a man gifted in the word to prophecy
     good.

For it will be better for England and all the world in a season,
     as I prophecy this day.

For I prophecy that they will obey the motions of the spirit
     descended upon them as at this day.

60.   For they have seen the glory of God already come down upon
     the trees.

For I prophecy that it will descend upon their heads also.

For I prophecy that the praise of God will be in every man's
     mouth in the Publick streets.

For I prophecy that there will be Publick worship in the cross
     ways and fields.

For I prophecy that the general salutation will be. The Lord
     Jesus prosper you. I wish you good luck in the name of
     the Lord Jesus.

Lines 108-113

For I prophecy that men will learn the use of their knees.

For every thing that can be done in that posture (upon the knees) is better so done than otherwise.

110. For I prophecy that they will understand the blessing and virtue of the rain.

For rain is exceedingly good for the human body.

For it is good therefore to have flat roofs to the houses, as of old.

For it is good to let the rain come upon the naked body unto purity and refreshment.

A SONG TO DAVID

London, 1763 [text].

DAVID the Son of JESSE said, and the MAN who was RAISED UP ON HIGH, the ANOINTED OF THE GOD OF JACOB, and the SWEET PSALMIST OF ISRAEL, said, The SPIRIT OF THE LORD spake by ME, and HIS WORD was in my TONGUE. 2 Sam. xxiii. 1, 2

Contents.

Invocation, ver. 1, 2, 3.—The excellence and lustre of David's character in twelve points of view, ver. 4; proved from the history of his life, to ver. 17.—He consecrates his genius for consolation and edification.— The subjects he made choice of—the Supreme Being—angels; men of renown; the works of nature in all directions, either particularly or collectively considered, to ver. 27.—He obtains power over infernal spirits, and the malignity of his enemies; wins the heart of Michal, to ver. 30.—Shews that the pillars of knowledge are the monuments of God's works in the first week, to ver. 38.—An exercise upon the decalogue, from ver. 40 to 49.—The transcendent virtue of praise and adoration, ver. 50 and 51.—An exercise upon the seasons, and the right use of them, from ver. 52 to 64.—An exercise upon the senses, and how to subdue them, from ver. 65 to 71 —An amplification in five degrees, which is wrought up to this conclusion, That the best poet which ever lived was thought worthy of the highest honour which possibly can be conceived, as *the Saviour of the world was ascribed to his house, and called his son in the body.*   Christopher Smart

I

O THOU, that sit'st upon a throne,
With harp of high majestic tone,
    To praise the King of kings;
And voice of heav'n-ascending swell,
Which, while its deeper notes excell,
    Clear, as a clarion, rings:

II

To bless each valley, grove and coast,
And charm the cherubs to the post
    Of gratitude in throngs;
To *keep* the days on Zion's mount,
And send the year to his account,
    With dances and with songs:

III

O Servant of God's holiest charge,
The minister of praise at large,
    Which thou may'st now receive;
From thy blest mansion hail and hear,
From topmost eminence appear
    To this the wreath I weave.

IV

Great, valiant, pious, good, and clean,
Sublime, contemplative, serene,
    Strong, constant, pleasant, wise!
Bright effluence of exceeding grace;
Best man!—the swiftness and the race,
    The peril, and the prize!

V

Great—from the lustre of his crown,
From Samuel's horn and God's renown,
    Which is the people's voice;
For all the host, from rear to van,
Applauded and embrac'd the man—
    The man of God's own choice.

VI

Valiant—the word and up he rose—
The fight—he triumph'd o'er the foes,
  Whom God's just laws abhor;
And arm'd in gallant faith he took
Against the boaster, from the brook,
  The weapons of the war.

VII

Pious—magnificent and grand;
'Twas he the famous temple plan'd:
  (The seraph in his soul)
Foremost to give the Lord his dues,
Foremost to bless the welcome news,
  And foremost to condole.

VIII

Good—from Jehudah's genuine vein,
From God's best nature good in grain,
  His aspect and his heart;
To pity, to forgive, to save,
Witness En-gedi's conscious cave,
  And Shimei's blunted dart.

IX

Clean—if perpetual prayer be pure,
And love, which could itself innure
  To fasting and to fear—
Clean in his gestures, hands, and feet,
To smite the lyre, the dance compleat,
  To play the sword and spear.

X

Sublime—invention ever young,
Of vast conception, tow'ring tongue,
  To God th'eternal theme;
Notes from yon exaltations caught,
Unrival'd royalty of thought,
  O'er meaner strains supreme.

XI

Contemplative—on God to fix
His musings, and above the six
　　The sabbath-day he blest;
'Twas then his thoughts self-conquest prun'd,
And heavenly melancholy tun'd,
　　To bless and bear the rest.

XII

Serene—to sow the seeds of peace,
Rememb'ring, when he watch'd the fleece,
　　How sweetly Kidron purl'd—
To further knowledge, silence vice,
And plant perpetual paradise
　　When God had calm'd the world.

XIII

Strong—in the Lord, who could defy
Satan, and all his powers that lie
　　In sempiternal night;
And hell, and horror, and despair
Were as the lion and the bear
　　To his undaunted might.

XIV

Constant—in love to God THE TRUTH,
Age, manhood, infancy and youth—
　　To Jonathan his friend
Constant, beyond the verge of death;
And Ziba, and Mephibosheth,
　　His endless fame attend.

XV

Pleasant—and various as the year;
Man, soul, and angel, without peer,
　　Priest, champion, sage and boy;
In armour, or in ephod clad,
His pomp, his piety was glad;
　　Majestic was his joy.

XVI

Wise—in recovery from his fall,
Whence rose his eminence o'er all,
 Of all the most revil'd;
The light of Israel in his ways,
Wise are his precepts, prayer and praise,
 And counsel to his child.

XVII

His muse, bright angel of his verse,
Gives balm for all the thorns that pierce,
 For all the pangs that rage;
Blest light, still gaining on the gloom,
The more than Michal of his bloom,
 Th' Abishag of his age.

XVIII

He sung of God—the mighty source
Of all things—the stupendous force
 On which all strength depends;
From whose right arm, beneath whose eyes,
All period, pow'r, and enterprize
 Commences, reigns, and ends.

XIX

Angels—their ministry and meed,
Which to and fro with blessings speed,
 Or with their citterns wait;
Where Michael with his millions bows,
Where dwells the seraph and his spouse,
 The cherub and her mate.

XX

Of man—the semblance and effect
Of God and Love—the Saint elect
 For infinite applause—
To rule the land, the briny broad,
To be laborious in his laud,
 And heroes in his cause.

XXI

The world—the clustring spheres he made,
The glorious light, the soothing shade,
   Dale, champaign, grove, and hill;
The multitudinous abyss,
Where secrecy remains in bliss,
   And wisdom hides her skill.

XXII

Trees, plants, and flow'rs—of virtuous root;
Gem yielding blossom, yielding fruit,
   Choice gums and precious balm;
Bless ye the nosegay in the vale,
And with the sweetners of the gale
   Enrich the thankful psalm.

XXIII

Of fowl—e'en ev'ry beak and wing
Which chear the winter, hail the spring,
   That live in peace and prey;
They that make music, or that mock,
The quail, the brave domestic cock,
   The raven, swan, and jay.

XXIV

Of fishes—ev'ry size and shape,
Which nature frames of light escape,
   Devouring man to shun:
The shells are in the wealthy deep,
The shoals upon the surface leap,
   And love the glancing sun.

XXV

Of beasts—the beaver plods his task;
While the sleek tygers roll and bask,
   Nor yet the shades arouse:
Her cave the mining coney scoops;
Where o'er the mead the mountain stoops,
   The kids exult and brouse.

XXVI

Of gems—their virtue and their price,
Which hid in earth from man's device,
    Their darts of lustre sheathe;
The jasper of the master's stamp,
The topaz blazing like a lamp
    Among the mines beneath.

XXVII

Blest was the tenderness he felt
When to his graceful harp he knelt,
    And did for audience call;
When satan with his hand he quell'd,
And in serene suspence he held
    The frantic throes of Saul.

XXVIII

His furious foes no more malign'd
As he such melody divin'd,
    And sense and soul detain'd;
Now striking strong, now soothing soft,
He sent the godly sounds aloft,
    Or in delight refrain'd.

XXIX

When up to heav'n his thoughts he pil'd,
From fervent lips fair Michal smil'd,
    As blush to blush she stood;
And chose herself the queen, and gave
Her utmost from her heart, 'so brave,
    And plays his hymns so good.'

XXX

The pillars of the Lord are seven,
Which stand from earth to topmost heav'n;
    His wisdom drew the plan;
His WORD accomplish'd the design,
From brightest gem to deepest mine,
    From CHRIST enthron'd to man.

XXXI

Alpha, the cause of causes, first
In station, fountain, whence the burst
   Of light, and blaze of day;
Whence bold attempt, and brave advance,
Have motion, life, and ordinance,
   And heav'n itself its stay.

XXXII

Gamma supports the glorious arch
On which angelic legions march,
   And is with sapphires pav'd;
Thence the fleet clouds are sent adrift,
And thence the painted folds, that lift
   The crimson veil, are wav'd.

XXXIII

Eta with living sculpture breathes,
With verdant carvings, flow'ry wreathes
   Of never-wasting bloom;
In strong relief his goodly base
All instruments of labour grace,
   The trowel, spade, and loom.

XXXIV

Next Theta stands to the Supreme—
Who form'd, in number, sign, and scheme,
   Th' illustrious lights that are;
And one address'd his saffron robe,
And one, clad in a silver globe,
   Held rule with ev'ry star.

XXXV

Iota's tun'd to choral hymns
Of those that fly, while he that swims
   In thankful safety lurks;
And foot, and chapitre, and niche,
The various histories enrich
   Of God's recorded works.

XXXVI

Sigma presents the social droves,
With him that solitary roves,
　　And man of all the chief;
Fair on whose face, and stately frame,
Did God impress his hallow'd name,
　　For ocular belief.

XXXVII

OMEGA! GREATEST and the BEST,
Stands sacred to the day of rest,
　　For gratitude and thought;
Which bless'd the world upon his pole,
And gave the universe his goal,
　　And clos'd th'infernal draught.

XXXVIII

O DAVID, scholar of the Lord!
Such is thy science, whence reward
　　And infinite degree;
O strength, O sweetness, lasting ripe!
God's harp thy symbol, and thy type
　　The lion and the bee!

XXXIX

There is but One who ne'er rebell'd,
But One by passion unimpell'd,
　　By pleasures unintice't;
He from himself his semblance sent,
Grand object of his own content,
　　And saw the God in CHRIST.

XL

Tell them I am, JEHOVA said
To MOSES: while earth heard in dread,
　　And smitten to the heart,
At once above, beneath, around,
All nature, without voice or sound,
　　Replied, O Lord, THOU ART.

XLI

Thou art—to give and to confirm,
For each his talent and his term;
    All flesh thy bounties share:
Thou shalt not call thy brother fool;
The porches of the Christian school
    Are meekness, peace, and pray'r.

XLII

Open, and naked of offence,
Man's made of mercy, soul, and sense;
    God arm'd the snail and wilk;
Be good to him that pulls thy plough;
Due food and care, due rest, allow
    For her that yields thee milk.

XLIII

Rise up before the hoary head,
And God's benign commandment dread,
    Which says thou shalt not die:
'Not as I will, but as thou wilt,'
Pray'd He whose conscience knew no guilt;
    With whose bless'd pattern vie.

XLIV

Use all thy passions!—love is thine,
And joy, and jealousy divine;
    Thine hope's eternal fort,
And care thy leisure to disturb,
With fear concupiscence to curb,
    And rapture to transport.

XLV

Act simply, as occasion asks;
Put mellow wine in season'd casks;
    Till not with ass and bull:
Remember thy baptismal bond;
Keep from commixtures foul and fond,
    Nor work thy flax with wool.

XLVI

Distribute: pay the Lord his tithe,
And make the widow's heart-strings blithe;
 Resort with those that weep:
As you from all and each expect,
For all and each thy love direct,
 And render as you reap.

XLVII

The slander and its bearer spurn,
And propagating praise sojourn
 To make thy welcome last;
Turn from old Adam to the New;
By hope futurity pursue;
 Look upwards to the past.

XLVIII

Controul thine eye, salute success,
Honour the wiser, happier bless,
 And for thy neighbour feel;
Grutch not of mammon and his leaven,
Work emulation up to heaven
 By knowledge and by zeal.

XLIX

O DAVID, highest in the list
Of worthies, on God's ways insist,
 *The genuine word repeat:
Vain are the documents of men,
And vain the flourish of the pen
 That keeps the fool's conceit.

L

PRAISE above all—for praise prevails;
Heap up the measure, load the scales,
 And good to goodness add:
The gen'rous soul her saviour aids,
But peevish obloquy degrades;
 The Lord is great and glad.

---

*Ps. 119. [Smart]

LI

For ADORATION all the ranks
Of angels yield eternal thanks,
   And DAVID in the midst;
With God's good poor, which, last and least
In man's esteem, thou to thy feast,
   O blessed bride-groom, bidst.

LII

For ADORATION seasons change,
And order, truth, and beauty range,
   Adjust, attract, and fill:
The grass the polyanthus cheques;
And polish'd porphyry reflects,
   By the descending rill.

LIII

Rich almonds colour to the prime
For ADORATION; tendrils climb,
   And fruit-trees pledge their gems;
And *Ivis with her gorgeous vest
Builds for her eggs her cunning nest,
   And bell-flowers bow their stems.

LIV

With vinous syrup cedars spout;
From rocks pure honey gushing out,
   For ADORATION springs:
All scenes of painting croud the map
Of nature; to the mermaid's pap
   The scaled infant clings.

LV

The spotted ounce and playsome cubs
Run rustling 'mongst the flow'ring shrubs,
   And lizards feed the moss;
For ADORATION beasts embark,
While waves upholding halcyon's ark
   No longer roar and toss.

---

*Humming-bird. [Smart]

LVI

While Israel sits beneath his fig,
With coral root and amber sprig
   The wean'd advent'rer sports;
Where to the palm the jasmin cleaves,
For ADORATION 'mongst the leaves
   The gale his peace reports.

LVII

Increasing days their reign exalt,
Nor in the pink and mottled vault
   Th'opposing spirits tilt;
And, by the coasting reader spied,
The silverlings and crusions glide
   For ADORATION gilt.

LVIII *summer*

For ADORATION rip'ning canes
And cocoa's purest milk detains
   The western pilgrim's staff;
Where rain in clasping boughs inclos'd,
And vines with oranges dispos'd,
   Embow'r the social laugh.

LIX

Now labour his reward receives,
For ADORATION counts his sheaves
   To peace, her bounteous prince;
The nectarine his strong tint imbibes,
And apples of ten thousand tribes,
   And quick peculiar quince.

LX

The wealthy crops of whit'ning rice,
'Mongst thyine woods and groves of spice,
   For ADORATION grow;
And, marshall'd in the fenced land,
The peaches and pomegranates stand,
   Where wild carnations blow.

— fall

LXI

The laurels with the winter strive;
The crocus burnishes alive
    Upon the snow-clad earth:
For ADORATION myrtles stay
To keep the garden from dismay,
    And bless the sight from dearth.

LXII

The pheasant shows his pompous neck;
And ermine, jealous of a speck,
    With fear eludes offence:
The sable, with his glossy pride,
For ADORATION is descried,
    Where frosts the wave condense.

LXIII

The chearful holly, pensive yew,
And holy thorn, their trim renew;
    The squirrel hoards his nuts:
All creatures batten o'er their stores,
And careful nature all her doors
    For ADORATION shuts.

LXIV

For ADORATION, DAVID's psalms
Lift up the heart to deeds of alms;
    And he, who kneels and chants,
Prevails his passions to controul,
Finds meat and med'cine to the soul,
    Which for translation pants.

LXV

For ADORATION, beyond match,
The scholar bulfinch aims to catch
    The soft flute's iv'ry touch;
And, careless on the hazle spray,
The daring redbreast keeps at bay
    The damsel's greedy clutch.

LXVI

For ADORATION, in the skies,
The Lord's philosopher espies
    The Dog, the Ram, and Rose;
The planet's ring, Orion's sword;
Nor is his greatness less ador'd
    In the vile worm that glows.

LXVII

For ADORATION* on the strings
The western breezes work their wings,
    The captive ear to sooth.—
Hark! 'tis a voice—how still, and small—
That makes the cataracts to fall,
    Or bids the sea be smooth.

LXVIII

For ADORATION, incense comes
From bezoar, and Arabian gums;
    And on the civet's furr.
But as for prayer, or e're it faints,
Far better is the breath of saints
    Than galbanum and myrrh.

LXIX

For ADORATION from the down,
Of dam'sins to th'anana's crown,
    God sends to tempt the taste;
And while the luscious zest invites
The sense, that in the scene delights,
    Commands desire be chaste.

LXX

For ADORATION, all the paths
Of grace are open, all the baths
    Of purity refresh;
And all the rays of glory beam
To deck the man of God's esteem,
    Who triumphs o'er the flesh.

---

*Æolian harp. [Smart]

LXXI

For ADORATION, in the dome
Of Christ the sparrows find an home;
 And on his olives perch:
The swallow also dwells with thee,
O man of God's humility,
 Within his Saviour CHURCH.

LXXII

Sweet is the dew that falls betimes,
And drops upon the leafy limes;
 Sweet Hermon's fragrant air:
Sweet is the lilly's silver bell,
And sweet the wakeful tapers smell
 That watch for early pray'r.

LXXIII

Sweet the young nurse with love intense,
Which smiles o'er sleeping innocence;
 Sweet when the lost arrive:
Sweet the musician's ardour beats,
While his vague mind's in quest of sweets,
 The choicest flow'rs to hive.

LXXIV

Sweeter in all the strains of love,
The language of thy turtle dove,
 Pair'd to thy swelling chord;
Sweeter with ev'ry grace endu'd,
The glory of thy gratitude,
 Respir'd unto the Lord.

LXXV

Strong is the horse upon his speed;
Strong in pursuit the rapid glede,
 Which makes at once his game:
Strong the tall ostrich on the ground;
Strong thro' the turbulent profound
 Shoots *xiphias to his aim.

---

*The sword-fish. [Smart]

LXXVI

Strong is the lion—like a coal
His eye-ball—like a bastion's mole
 His chest against the foes:
Strong, the gier-eagle on his sail,
Strong against tide, th'enormous whale
 Emerges as he goes.

LXXVII

But stronger still, in earth and air,
And in the sea, the man of pray'r;
 And far beneath the tide;
And in the seat of faith assign'd,
Where ask is have, where seek is find,
 Where knock is open wide.

LXXVIII

Beauteous the fleet before the gale;
Beauteous the multitudes in mail,
 Rank'd arms and crested heads:
Beauteous the garden's umbrage mild,
Walk, water, meditated wild,
 And all the bloomy beds.

LXXIX

Beauteous the moon full on the lawn;
And beauteous, when the veil's withdrawn,
 The virgin to her spouse:
Beauteous the temple deck'd and fill'd,
When to the heav'n of heav'ns they build
 Their heart-directed vows.

LXXX

Beauteous, yea beauteous more than these,
The shepherd king upon his knees,
 For his momentous trust;
With wish of infinite conceit,
For man, beast, mute, the small and great,
 And prostrate dust to dust.

LXXXI

Precious the bounteous widow's mite;
And precious, for extream delight,
   *The largess from the churl:
Precious the ruby's blushing blaze,
And †alba's blest imperial rays,
   And pure cerulean pearl.

LXXXII

Precious the penitential tear;
And precious is the sigh sincere,
   Acceptable to God:
And precious are the winning flow'rs,
In gladsome Israel's feast of bow'rs,
   Bound on the hallow'd sod.

LXXXIII

More precious that diviner part
Of David, ev'n the Lord's own heart,
   Great, beautiful, and new:
In all things where it was intent,
In all extreams, in each event,
   Proof—answ'ring true to true.

LXXXIV

Glorious the sun in mid career;
Glorious th'assembled fires appear;
   Glorious the comet's train:
Glorious the trumpet and alarm;
Glorious th'almighty stretch'd-out arm;
   Glorious th'enraptur'd main:

LXXXV

Glorious the northern lights astream;
Glorious the song, when God's the theme;
   Glorious the thunder's roar:
Glorious hosanna from the den;
Glorious the catholic amen;
   Glorious the martyr's gore:

---

*Sam. xxv 18. [Smart. I.e. 1 Sam. xxv 18.].
†Rev. xi 17. [Smart. A mistake for Rev. ii 17].

LXXXVI

Glorious—more glorious is the crown
Of Him that brought salvation down
    By meekness, call'd thy Son;
Thou at stupendous truth believ'd,
And now the matchless deed's atchiev'd,
    DETERMINED, DARED, and DONE.

ODE TO ADMIRAL SIR GEORGE POCOCK
From *Poems. By Mr Smart.*
London, 1763 [text].

When CHRIST, the seaman, was aboard
    Swift as an arrow to the *White*,
While Ocean his rude rapture roar'd,
    *The vessel gain'd the Haven with delight:
We therefore first to him the song renew,
Then sing of POCOCK's praise, and make the point in view.

The Muse must humble e're she rise,
    And kneel to kiss her Master's feet,
Thence at one spring she mounts the skies
    And in *New Salem* vindicates her seat;
Seeks to the temple of th' Angelic choir,
And hoists the ENGLISH FLAG upon the topmost spire.

O Blessed of the Lord of Hosts,
    In either India most renown'd,
The Echo of the Eastern coasts,
    And all th' Atlantic shores thy name resound.—
The victor's clemency, the seaman's art,
The cool delib'rate head, and warm undaunted heart.

---

*John vi. 21. [Smart]

My pray'r was with Thee, when thou sail'd
    With prophecies of sure success;
My thanks to Heav'n, that thou prevail'd
    Shall last as long as I can breathe or bless;
And built upon thy deeds my song shall tow'r,
And swell, as it ascends, in spirit and in pow'r.

There is no thunder half so loud,
    As God's applauses in the height,
For those, that have his name avow'd,
    Ev'n *Christian* Patriots valorous and great;
Who for the general welfare stand or fall,
And have no sense of self, and know no dread at all.

Amongst the numbers lately fir'd
    To act upon th' heroic plan,
Grace has no worthier chief inspir'd,
    Than that sublime, insuperable man,
Who could th' out-numb'ring *French* so oft defeat,
And from th' HAVANNAH stor'd his brave victorious fleet.

And yet how silent his return
    With scarce a welcome to his place—
Stupidity and unconcern,
    Were settled in each voice and on each face.
As private as myself he walk'd along,
Unfavour'd by a friend, unfollow'd by the throng.

Thy triumph, therefore, is not here,
    Thy glories for a while postpon'd,
The hero shines not in his sphere,
    But where the Author of all worth is own'd.—
Where *Patience* still persists to praise and pray
For all the Lord bestows, and all he *takes away*.

Nor HOWARD, FORBISHER, or DRAKE,
    Or VERNON's fam'd *Herculean* deed;

Not all the miracles of BLAKE,
    Can the great Chart of thine exploits exceed.—
Then rest upon thyself and dwell secure,
And cultivate the arts, and feed th'*increasing* poor.

O NAME accustom'd and innur'd
    To fame and hardship round the globe,
For which fair Honour has insur'd
    The warrior's truncheon, and the consul's robe;
Who still the more is *done* and *understood*,
Art easy of access, art affable and good.

O NAME acknowledged and rever'd
    Where ISIS plays her pleasant stream,
When'er thy tale is read or heard,
    The good shall bless thee, and the wise esteem;
And they, whose offspring* lately felt thy care,
Shall in TEN THOUSAND CHURCHES make their daily pray'r.—

'Connubial bliss and homefelt joy,
    And ev'ry social praise be thine;
Plant thou the oak, the poor employ;
    Or plans of vast benevolence design;
And speed, when CHRIST his servant shall release,
From triumph over death to everlasting peace.'

———

*Alluding to the Admiral's noble Benefaction to the Sons of the Clergy. [Smart].

ON A BED OF GUERNSEY LILIES
Written in September 1763.
From *Ode to the Right Honourable the Earl of Northumberland.*
London, 1764 [text].

        Ye beauties! O how great the sum
            Of sweetness that ye bring;
        On what a charity ye come
            To bless the latter spring!

How kind the visit that ye pay,
Like strangers on a rainy day,
   When heartiness despair'd of guests:
No neighbour's praise your pride alarms,
No rival flow'r surveys your charms,
   Or heightens, or contests!

Lo, thro' her works gay nature grieves
   How brief she is and frail,
As ever o'er the falling leaves
   Autumnal winds prevail.
Yet still the philosophic mind
Consolatory food can find,
   And hope her anchorage maintain:
We never are deserted quite;
'Tis by succession of delight
   That love supports his reign.

ON GRATITUDE
To the Memory of Mr Seaton.

O Muse! O Music! Voice & Lyre,
   Which are together Psalm of Praise
From heav'n the kneeling bard inspire
   New thoughts, new grace of utt'rance raise,
That more acceptable with Thee
   We thy best service may begin
O thou that bent thine hallow'd knee,
   And bless'd to bleed for Adam's sin.
Then did the Spirit of a Man
   Above all height sublimely towr,
And then sweet Gratitude began
   To claim Supremacy from Pow'r.
But how shall we those steps ascend
   By which the Host approach the Throne?

Love thou thy brother & thy friend,
    Whom thou on earth has seen & known.
For Gratitude may make the *plea
    Of Love by Sisterhood most dear—
How can we reach the first degree
    If we neglect a step so near?
So shall we take dear *Seaton*'s part
    When paths of topmost heav'n are trod,
And pay the talent of our heart
    Thrown up ten thousand fold to God.
He knew the art the World dispise
    Might to his merit be applied
Who when for man he left the skies
    By all was hated, scorn'd, denied.
†'The man that gives me thanks & laud
    Does honour to my glorious name'
Thus God did David's works applaud,
    And seal'd for everlasting fame.
And this for SEATON shall redound
    To praise, as long as *Camus* runs;
Sure Gratitude by him was crown'd,
    Who bless'd her Maker & her Sons.
When *Spencer* virtuous *Sydney* prais'd
    When *Prior Dorsett* hail'd to heav'n;
They more by Gratitude were rais'd
    Than all the *Nine* & all the *Sev'n*.
Then, O ye emulative tribe
    Of Granta, strains divine persue;
The glory to the Lord ascribe,
    Yet honour *Seaton*'s memory too.
The Throne of Excellence accost
    And be the post of Pray'r maintain'd;
For Paradise had ne'er been lost
    Had heav'nly Gratitude remain'd.

---

*I John iv. 20.   †Psalm l. 23. [Smart]

Lyrics from HANNAH, AN ORATORIO
London, 1764 [text].

Act I, p. 7.

> Is not Genius heav'nly Fire,
>> Thoughts so great and Words so free,
> Heighten'd on the living Lyre
>> Giv'n from God and giv'n to Thee?
> Are not these the way to Fame
>> Tow'ring from th'immortal Page,
> Is not *Hannah* then a Name
>> Glorious to the latest Age?

Act I, p. 8.

> There is no Part of Heav'n so high,
>> But is accessible with ease,
> If faithful Diligence apply
>> Upon her never-wearied Knees.
> By Pray'r the Miracle is done,
> By Pray'r th' eternal Prize is won.

> But if with Lips and Heart in tune
>> The Lute's soft Symphonies unite,
> Sweet Hymnist, thou must have thy Boon
>> Or Heav'n itself shall lose its Light.
> By Pray'r the Miracle is done,
> By Pray'r th' eternal Prize is won.

Act II, p. 12.

> Every Bird that pipes a Note,
> Every Shrub that bears a Bloom,
>> Thine Unkindnesses upbraid;
> Grateful is the Linnet's Throat,
> Grateful is the Bay's Perfume,
>> And to God their Tribute's paid.

> But the Monster of our Scorn,
> He whom Men and Angels hate,

And ev'n Heathen Schools despise;
(Better had he ne'er been born)
Is that odious base Ingrate,
   Who his God and Truth denies.

Act II, p. 14.

   Female Tempers ebb and flow,
      With the Bounty of their Lovers;
Spirits never are so low,
      But a Gift their State recovers.

   Sparing Hands and niggard Hearts,
      Are the Source of true Dejection;
He that all his Wealth imparts,
      Yields Endearment in Perfection.

A TRANSLATION OF THE PSALMS OF DAVID
Attempted in the Spirit of Christianity, and Adapted to the Divine Service
London, 1765 [text].

Psalm CIV

   Bless thou the Lord, my soul—how great,
O Lord, what a stupendous weight
   Of honours crown thy name;
Thou'rt cloath'd with majesty and might,
And glories how exceeding bright
   Come clust'ring on thy fame!

With light, which thou hast purer made,
As with a robe thou art array'd,
   Whose pow'r the world upholds;
And hang'st the skies in beauteous blue,
Wav'd like a curtain to the view,
   Down heav'n's high dome in folds.

His chamber-beams in floods he shrouds,
His chariots are the rolling clouds
   Upon th' etherial arch;
And on the rapid winds their wings
Majestical, the king of kings
   Walks in his awful march.

The guardian spirits know their post,
His heralds are th' angelic host
   Obedient to his will;
The delegated lightnings fly,
And flames are sent on embassy
   His mandates to fulfill.

Fair and full-finished at her birth,
Firm at the first he fixt the earth,
   And wrought her bases fast;
Her deep foundations has he girt,
That as the lively springs exert,
   Her state of rest might last.

Upon the surface deep and wide
Thou pouredst out the flowing tide,
   Like some loose garment spread;
The rising waters stood around,
And swoln above the level ground,
   O'ertop the mountain's head.

But at the thunder of thy word
Their inundations were deterr'd,
   And thy rebuke obey'd;
And to the centre from the top,
Th' unfathom'd ocean to a drop
   Was pacify'd and laid.

Then up into the hills they go,
And down upon the vales below

Again their way they find;
Till at such places they abide,
And in those due directions glide
 Thy wisdom has assign'd.

Thou over-rul'st the liquid mass,
And in the bounds they may not pass
 Thou shalt their floods restrain;
The way that is prescribed they learn
For ever, nor shall they return
 To cover earth again.

The living springs at his command
Are sent a succour to the land,
 For rivers the resource;
Which as by stooping woods they curve
'Mongst intermingl'd hills preserve
 Their interrupted course.

All beasts that haunt the distant groves,
Frequent the lucid stream in droves,
 As need and nature rule,
And asses of the wild, assuage
Their thirst, and the meridian age
 Of sultry sun-beams cool.

Near them thro' blossoms bursting ripe
The birds upon the perches pipe,
 As boughs the herbage shield;
And while each other they salute,
The trees from every quiv'ring shoot,
 Melodious musick yield.

He from his chambers dew distills,
And waters with his rain the hills
 Where'er their summits soar;
The vales, with sweet luxuriance clad,

Make all the face of nature glad
　　With never-failing store.

He laid the verdant turf to graze,
That earth the due supplies might raise
　　Of annual food and wealth;
And fragrant herbs and flow'rs profuse
The seasons on the field produce
　　For pleasure and for health.

He planted on the rock the vine,
To glad the heart of man with wine,
　　And crown the thankful bowl;
And to exhilarate the face,
He gave the cruise, and broke in grace
　　His bread sustains the soul.

The trees with precious balsam sweat,
Which GRACE in seemly rows has set
　　By her almighty pow'r;
And Lebanon, which God perfumes,
His crest with stately cedar plumes,
　　Whose tufted tops embow'r.

The feather'd families of air
Contrive their cunning fabricks there,
　　What time the sexes mix;
The storks for elevation seek
To loftier firs with bolder beak
　　Their pensile house to fix.

The kid that brouses on the thyme,
Looks from the precipice sublime,
　　And every peril braves;
The skulking connies dwell secure,
And for defence their young immure
　　In quarries and in caves.

He taught the silver moon her way,
Her monthly and nocturnal sway,
　　Where'er she wanes or grows;
The glorious globe that gilds the skies
Is conscious of his early rise,
　　And his descent he knows.

The lines of light and shade to mark
Is thine, thou bidst the night be dark,
　　Beneath whose solemn gloom
The forest-beasts forsake their den,
And all that shun the walks of men,
　　Their wonted haunts resume.

The lions rouse to fill the scene,
With eyes of baleful lightning keen
　　Upon the desart rude;
And as in surly-sounding tone
They make the hollow caverns groan,
　　From God require their food.

But at the glancing of the dawn,
Ere yet the sun-beams o'er the lawn
　　The burnish'd orb unveil;
Alarm'd they flee their nightly round,
And in their place with peace profound
　　Their weary'd limbs regale.

While man, frail nature to sustain,
Awakes to labour and to pain,
　　Till from the wish'd-for west
Th' approaches of the dusky eve
Give to his toil a short reprieve,
　　And send him home to rest.

How manifold thy works are made,
O Lord—by thankful man survey'd,

What an exhaustless theme!
In wisdom didst thou all dispense,
How with thy vast munificence
    Heav'n, earth, air, all things teem!

So does the sea, whose shelvy rocks
And depths with numberless he stocks
    From life's eternal fount;
Some in the nether crannies skulk,
And some of huge enormous bulk
    The swelling floods surmount.

There go the ships from shore to shore,
Of distant climes the diff'rent store
    To take and to discharge;
There that Leviathan resorts,
Which at thy blessed bidding sports
    At leisure and at large.

All these upon thy love depend,
And on thy providence attend
    Their daily wants to urge;
And as the stated hour revolves,
The bread is broke, the dew dissolves
    Upon the rising surge.

They gather that which is diffus'd,
Nor ought is wasted or abus'd,
    So has thy wisdom will'd;
Thy bounteous hand prepares a feast,
And all from greatest to the least
    Thou fillest, and they're fill'd.

Thou hid'st thy face—however brief
Thy absence, it is instant grief
    Of infinite degree;
'Tis thine to give, and to withdraw

Their breath, and by a stablish'd law
    They are, or cease to be.

But by succession they survive,
And sense and pow'r to move derive,
    As from thy spirit sent;
Anew their moulded dust is warm'd—
Ev'n earth herself by thee reform'd,
    Shall other scenes present.

The glorious majesty and love
Of God shall have no bounds, above
    All mortal change and chance;
The Lord shall heav'n's whole choir employ
In anthems of exceeding joy
    To see his works advance.

Abash'd at his tremendous look,
The earth with strong commotions shook,
    Which all her awe bespoke;
He touch'd the hills, their summits nod,
And at the weighty hand of God
    They totter, and they smoke.

That goodness which these years prolongs,
Shall give new spirit to my songs
    As measure to my span;
While I my life and limbs possess,
The bounteous author will I bless
    With all the might of man.

As in the spirit I repeat
His praise, my musings shall be sweet,
    To just refinement wrought;
Yea, while I yet suppress my voice,
To thee, O Lord, will I rejoice
    In melody of thought.

The men, by carnal sins entic'd,
Must fall before the rod of Christ,
 Confounded and amaz'd;—
Praise thou the Lord, my soul apart—
Praise ye, who hear with voice and heart—
 The Lord our God be prais'd.

Psalm CXXVII

If the work be not direct,
 And the Lord the fabrick build,
All the plans that men project
 Are but labour idly spill'd.

If the Lord be not the guard,
 And the forts and tow'rs sustain,
All the city gates are barr'd,
 And the watchman wakes in vain.

Vainly for the bread of care
 Late and early hours ye keep,
For 'tis thus by fervent pray'r
 That he lays the blest asleep.

Lo! thy children are not thine,
 Nor the fruits of female love,
But an heritage divine,
 And a blessing from above.

Like as arrows in the grasp
 Of a valiant man of might,
Are the children that you clasp
 In some future hour of fight.

Blest! who in his quiver stows
 Darts like these, a goodly freight,
Nor shall blush when with his foes
 He shall parley in the gate.

Psalm CXXXIV

Attend to the musick divine
 Ye people of God with the priest,
At once your Hosanna combine
 As meekly ye bow to the east.

Ye servants that look to the lights
 Which blaze in the house of the Lord,
And keep up the watch of the nights
 To bless each apartment and ward,

The holy of holies review,
 And lift up your hands with your voice,
And there sing your anthems anew,
 In praise to Jehova rejoice.

The Lord that made heav'n and earth,
 Which rules o'er the night and the day,
His blessing bestow on your mirth,
 And hear you whenever ye pray.

HYMNS AND SPIRITUAL SONGS FOR THE FASTS AND FESTIVALS OF THE CHURCH OF ENGLAND
From *A Translation of the Psalms of David.*
London, 1765 [text].

Te decet Hymnus

שירו לו זמרו לו שיחו בכל
נפלאתיו

Hymn 1
New Year.

Word of endless adoration,
 Christ, I to thy call appear;
On my knees in meek prostration
 To begin a better year.

Spirits in eternal waiting,
　　*Special ministers of pray'r,
Which our welcome antedating,
　　Shall the benediction bear.

Which, the type of vows completed,
　　Shall the wreathed garland send,
While new blessings are intreated,
　　And communicants attend.

Emblem of the hopes beginning,
　　Who the budding rods shall bind,
Way from guiltless nature's winning,
　　In good-will to human kind.

Ye that dwell with cherub-turtles
　　Mated in that upmost light,
Or parade† amongst the myrtles,
　　On your steeds of speckl'd white.

Ye that sally from the portal
　　Of yon everlasting bow'rs,
Sounding symphonies immortal,
　　Years, and months, and days, and hours.

But nor myrtles, nor the breathing
　　Of the never-dying grove,
Nor the chaplets sweetly wreathing,
　　And by hands angelic wove;

Not the musick or the mazes
　　Of those spirits aptly tim'd,
Can avail like pray'r and praises
　　By the Lamb himself sublim'd.

---

*Tobit xxii. 15. [Smart. An error for Tobit xii. 15] .
†Zec. i. 8. [Smart] .

Take ye therefore what ye give him,
    Of his fulness grace for grace,
Strive to think him, speak him, live him,
    Till you find him face to face.

Sing like David, or like Hannah,
    As the spirit first began,
To the God of heights hosanna!
    Peace and charity to man.

Christ his blessing universal
    On th' arch-patriarch's seed bestow,
Which attend to my rehearsal
    Of melodious pray'r below.

Hymn II
Circumcision

When Abraham was bless'd,
And on his face profess'd
    The Saviour Christ hereafter born,
'Thou pilgrim and estrang'd,
Thy name, said God, is chang'd,
    Thy lot secur'd from want and scorn.

'O Abraham, my friend,
My covenant attend,
    Which Shilo's self shall not repeal,
Chastise from carnal sin
Thy house and all thy kin,
    Thy faith by circumcision seal.'

The promis'd Shilo came,
And then receiv'd the name
    Of Jesus, Saviour of the soul;
As he the law fulfill'd

Which checks the fleshly-will'd,
    And o'er the passion gives controul.

O clean and undefil'd!
Thou shalt not be beguil'd
    By youthful heat and female art,
To thee the strains belong
Of that mysterious song
    Where none but virgins bear a part.

Come every purer thought,
By which the mind is wrought
    From man's corruption, nature's dust;
Away each vain desire,
And all the fiends that fire
    The soul to base and filthy lust.

Ye swans that sail and lave
In Jordan's hallow'd wave,
    Ah sweet! ah pensive! ah serene!
Thou rose of maiden flush,
Like Joseph's guiltless blush,
    And herb of ever-grateful green;

Ye lilies of perfume,
That triumph o'er the loom,
    And gaudy greatness far outshine;
And thou the famous tree,
Whose name is chastity,
    And all the brilliants of the mine;

Ye doves of silver down
That plume the seraph's crown,
    All, all the praise of Jesus sing,
The joy of heav'n and earth,
And Christ's eternal worth,
    The pearl of God, the Father's ring.

Let elegance, the flow'r
Of words, in tune and pow'r,
    Find some device of cleanest choice
About that gem to place—
'This is my HEIR of GRACE,
    In whose perfections I rejoice.'

Hymn III
Epiphany

GRACE, thou source of each perfection,
    Favour from the height thy ray;
Thou the star of all direction,
    Child of endless truth and day.

Thou that bidst my cares be calmer,
    Lectur'd what to seek and shun,
Come and guide a western palmer
    To the Virgin and her Son.

Lo! I travel in the spirit,
    On my knees my course I steer
To the house of might and merit
    With humility and fear.

Poor at least as John or Peter
    I my vows alone prefer;
But the strains of love are sweeter
    Than the frankincense and myrrh.

Neither purse nor scrip I carry,
    But the books of life and pray'r;
Nor a staff my foe to parry,
    'Tis the cross of Christ I bear.

From a heart serene and pleasant
    'Midst unnumber'd ills I feel,

I will meekly bring my present,
    And with sacred verses kneel.

Muse, through Christ the Word, inventive
    Of the praise so greatly due;
Heav'nly gratitude retentive
    Of the bounties ever new.

Fill my heart with genuine treasures,
    Pour them out before his feet,
High conceptions, mystic measures,
    Springing strong and flowing sweet.

Come, ye creatures of thanksgiving,
    Which are harmoniz'd to bless,
Birds that warble for your living,
    Beasts with ways of love express.

Thou the shepherd's faithful fellow,
    As he lies by Cedron's stream,
Where soft airs and waters mellow
    Take their Saviour for their theme.

Thou too gaily grave domestic,
    With whose young fond childhood plays,
Held too mean for verse majestic,
    First with me thy Maker praise.

Brousing kids, and lambkins grazing,
    Colts and younglings of the drove,
Come with all your modes of praising,
    Bounding through the leafless grove.

Ye that skill the flow'rs to fancy,
    And in just assemblage sort,
Pluck the primrose, pluck the pansy,
    And your prattling troop exhort.

'Little men, in Jesus mighty,
    And ye maids that go alone,
Bodies chaste, and spirits flighty,
    Ere the world and guilt are known.

'Breath so sweet, and cheeks so rosy—
    Put your little hands to pray,
Take ye ev'ry one a posy,
    And away to Christ, away.'—

Youth, benevolence, and beauty,
    In your Saviour's praise agree,
Which this day receives our duty,
    Sitting on the virgin's knee.

That from this day's institution
    Ev'ry penitent in deed,
At his hour of retribution,
    As a child, through him may speed.

Hymn VI
The Presentation of Christ in the Temple
Preserver of the church, thy spouse,
    From sacrilege and wrong,
To whom the myriads pay their vows,
Give ear, and in my heart arouse
    The spirit of a nobler song.

When Hiero built, from David's plan,
    The house of godlike style,
And Solomon, the prosp'rous man,
Whose reign with wealth and fame began,
    O'erlaid with gold the glorious pile;

Great was the concourse of mankind
    The structure to review;

Such bulk with sweet proportion join'd
The labours of a vaster mind,
   In all directions grand and true.

And yet it was not true and grand
   The Godhead to contain;
By whom immensity is spann'd,
Which has eternal in his hand
   The globe of his supreme domain.

Tho' there the congregation knelt
   The daily debt to pay,
Tho' there superior glories dwelt,
Tho' there the host their blessings dealt,
   The highest GRACE was far away.

At length another fane arose,
   The fabrick of the poor;
And built by hardship midst her foes
One hand for work and one for blows,
   Made this stupendous blessing sure.

That God should in the world appear
   Incarnate—as a child—
That he should be presented here,
At once our utmost doubts to clear,
   And make our hearts with wonder wild.

Present ye therefore, on your knees,
   Hearts, hands resign'd and clean;
Ye poor and mean of all degrees,
If he will condescend and please
   To take at least what orphans glean—

I speak for all—for them that fly,
   And for the race that swim;
For all that dwell in moist and dry,

Beasts, reptiles, flow'rs and gems to vie
    When gratitude begins her hymn.

Praise him ye doves, and ye that pipe
    Ere buds begin to stir;
Ev'n every finch of every stripe,
And thou of filial love the type,
    O stork! that sit'st upon the fir.

Praise him thou sea, to whom he gave
    The shoal of active mutes;
(Fit tenants of thy roaring wave)
Who comes to still the fiends, that rave
    In oracles and school disputes.

By Jesus number'd all and priz'd,
    Praise him in dale and hill;
Ye beasts for use and peace devis'd,
And thou which patient and despis'd,
    Yet shalt a prophecy fulfill.

Praise him ye family that weave
    The crimson to be spread
There, where communicants receive,
And ye, that form'd the eye to grieve,
    Hid in green bush or wat'ry bed.

Praise him ye flow'rs that serve the swarm
    With honey for their cells;
Ere yet the vernal day is warm,
To call out millions to perform
    Their gambols on your cups and bells.

Praise him ye gems of lively spark,
    And thou the pearl of price;
In that great depth or caverns dark,
Nor yet are wrested from the mark,
    To serve the turns of pride and vice.

Praise him ye cherubs of his breast,
    The mercies of his love,
Ere yet from guile and hate profest,
The phenix makes his fragrant nest
    In his own paradise above.

Hymn IX
The Annunciation of the Blessed Virgin

O Purity, thou test
Of love amongst the blest,
How excellent thou art,
The Lord Jehovah's heart,
    Whose sweet attributes embrace,
    Every virtue, praise and grace.

Thou fair and good dispos'd,
'Midst glories undisclos'd,
Inspire the notes to play
Upon the virgin's day;
    High above all females nam'd,
    And by Gabriel's voice proclaim'd.

Glad herald, ever sent
Upon some blest event,
But never sped to men
On such a charge till then—
    When his Saviour's feet he kiss'd,
    To promulge his birth dismiss'd.

Hail mystery! thou source
Of nature's plainest course,
How much this work transcends
Thine usual means and ends—
    Wherefore call'd, we shall not spare
    Louder praise, and oft'ner pray'r.

But if the work be new,
So shou'd the song be too,
By every thought that's born
In freshness of the morn;
    Every flight of active wings,
    Every shift upon the strings.

To praise the mighty hand
By which the world was mann'd,
Which dealt to great and small
Their talents clear of all;
    Kind to kind by likeness linkt,
    Various all, and all distinct.

Praise him seraphic tone
Of instruments unknown,
High strains on golden wire,
Work'd by etherial fire;
    Blowing on unceasing chords,
    'King of kings, and lord of lords.'

Praise Hannah, of the three,
That sang in Mary's key;
With her that made her psalm
Beneath the bow'ring palm;
    With the dame—Bethulia's boast,
    Honour'd o'er th' Assyrian host.

Praise him faith, hope, and love
That tend Jehovah's dove;
By men from lust repriev'd,
As females best conceiv'd;
    To remount the man and muse
    Far above all earthly views.

Hymn XII
St Mark

Pull up the bell-flow'rs of the spring,
And let the budding greenwood ring
   With many a chearful song;
All blessing on the human race,
From CHRIST, evangelist of grace,
   To whom these strains belong.

To whom belong the tribes that vie
In what is musick to the eye,
   Whose voice is 'stoop to pray'—
While many colour'd tints attire
His fav'rites, like the golden wire,
   The beams on wind flow'rs play.

To whom belong the dress and airs
Of nature in her warbling pairs,
   And in her bloomy pride;
By whom the man of pray'r computes
His year, and estimates the fruits
   Of every time and tide.

To whom the sacred penman cries,
And as he heav'nwards lifts his eyes,
   With meekness kneels him down;
Then what inspiring truth indites,
His strengthen'd memory recites,
   The tale of God's renown.

O holy Mark! ordain'd in youth
To be historian of the truth
   From heav'ns first fountain brought;
And Christ his hand was on thy head,
To bless thee that thou should'st be read,
   And in his churches taught.

And tho', as Peter's scribe and son,
Thou mightst a charity have done
    To cover his disgrace;
Yet strictly charg'd thou wouldst not spare
At large the treason to declare,
    And in its order place.

Thus in the church, to cleanse our sin,
By fair confession we begin,
    And in thanksgiving end;
And they that have the Lord deny'd,
Must not come there the crime to hide,
    But promise to amend.

Then let us not this day refuse,
With joy to give the Christian dues
    To Lazars at the door;
'O for the name and love of Christ
Spare one poor dole from all your grist,
    One mite from all your store!'

And those that in by-places lurk,
Invite with overpay to work,
    Thy garner'd hay to fill;
And worship on the new mown sod,
And active to the Lord thy God,
    Keep lust and conscience still.

Hymn XIII
St Philip and St James

Now the winds are all composure,
    But the breath upon the bloom,
Blowing sweet o'er each inclosure,
    Grateful off'rings of perfume.

Tansy, calaminth and daisies,
    On the river's margin thrive;
And accompany the mazes
    Of the stream that leaps alive.

Muse, accordant to the season,
    Give the numbers life and air;
When the sounds and objects reason
    In behalf of praise and pray'r.

All the scenes of nature quicken,
    By the genial spirit fann'd;
And the painted beauties thicken
    Colour'd by the master's hand.

Earth her vigour repossessing
    As the blasts are held in ward;
Blessing heap'd and press'd on blessing,
    Yield the measure of the Lord.

Beeches, without order seemly,
    Shade the flow'rs of annual birth,
And the lily smiles supremely
    Mention'd by the Lord on earth.

Couslips seize upon the fallow,
    And the cardamine in white,
Where the corn-flow'rs join the mallow,
    Joy and health, and thrift unite.

Study sits beneath her arbour,
    By the bason's glossy side;
While the boat from out its harbour
    Exercise and pleasure guide.

Pray'r and praise be mine employment,
    Without grudging or regret,

Lasting life, and long enjoyment,
 Are not here, and are not yet.

Hark! aloud, the black-bird whistles,
 With surrounding fragrance blest,
And the goldfinch in the thistles
 Makes provision for her nest.

Ev'n the hornet hives his honey,
 Bluecap builds his stately dome,
And the rocks supply the coney
 With a fortress and an home.

But the servants of their Saviour,
 Which with gospel-peace are shod,
Have no bed but what the paviour
 Makes them in the porch of God.

O thou house that hold'st the charter
 Of salvation from on high,
Fraught with prophet, saint, and martyr,
 Born to weep, to starve and die!

Great to-day thy song and rapture
 In the choir of Christ and WREN
When two prizes were the capture
 Of the hand that fish'd for men.

To the man of quick compliance
 Jesus call'd, and Philip came;
And began to make alliance
 For his master's cause and name.

James, of title most illustrious,
 Brother of the Lord, allow'd;
In the vineyard how industrious,
 Nor by years nor hardship bow'd!

Each accepted in his trial,
    One the CHEERFUL one the JUST;
Both of love and self-denial,
    Both of everlasting trust.

Living they dispens'd salvation,
    Heav'n-endow'd with grace and pow'r;
And they dy'd in imitation
    Of their Saviour's final hour.

Who, for cruel traitors pleading,
    Triumph'd in his parting breath;
O'er all miracles preceding
    His inestimable death.

Hymn XIX
The Nativity of St John the Baptist
    Great and bounteous BENEFACTOR,
        We thy gen'rous aid adjure,
    Shield us from the foul exactor,
        And his sons, that grind the poor.

    Lo the swelling fruits of summer,
        With inviting colours dy'd,
    Hang, for ev'ry casual comer,
        O'er the fence projecting wide.

    See the corn for plenty waving,
        Where the lark secur'd her eggs—
    In the spirit then be saving,
        Give the poor that sings and begs.

    Gentle nature seems to love us
        In each fair and finish'd scene,
    All is beauteous blue above us,
        All beneath is cheerful green.

Now when warmer rays enlighten
    And adorn the lengthen'd time,
When the views around us brighten,
    Days a rip'ning from their prime,

She that was as barren reckon'd,
    Had her course completely run,
And her dumb-struck husband beckon'd
    For a pen to write a son.

JOHN, the child of Zacharias,
    Just returning to this earth,
Prophet of the Lord Messias,
    And fore-runner of his birth.

He too martyr'd, shall precede him,
    Ere he speed to heav'n again,
Ere the traitors shall implead him,
    And the priest his God arraign.

John beheld the great and holy,
    Hail'd the love of God supreme;
O how gracious, meek, and lowly,
    When baptiz'd in Jordan's stream!

If from honour so stupendous
    He the grace of pow'r deriv'd,
And to tyrants was tremendous,
    That at fraud and filth conniv'd;

If he led a life of rigour,
    And th' abstemious vow obey'd;
If he preach'd with manly vigour,
    Practis'd sinners to dissuade;

If his voice by fair confession
    Christ's supremacy avow'd;

If he checked with due suppression
    Self-incitements to be proud.

Vice conspiring to afflict him
    To the death that ends the great,
Offer'd him a worthy victim
    For acceptance in the height.

Hymn XXXII
The Nativity of Our Lord and Saviour Jesus Christ
    Where is this stupendous stranger,
        Swains of Solyma, advise,
    Lead me to my Master's manger,
        Shew me where my Saviour lies?

O Most Mighty! O MOST HOLY!
    Far beyond the seraph's thought,
Art thou then so mean and lowly
    As unheeded prophets taught?

O the magnitude of meekness!
    Worth from worth immortal sprung;
O the strength of infant weakness,
    If eternal is so young!

If so young and thus eternal,
    Michael tune the shepherd's reed,
Where the scenes are ever vernal,
    And the loves be love indeed!

See the God blasphem'd and doubted
    In the schools of Greece and Rome;
See the pow'rs of darkness routed,
    Taken at their utmost gloom.

Nature's decorations glisten
 Far above their usual trim;
Birds on box and laurel listen,
 As so near the cherubs hymn.

Boreas now no longer winters
 On the desolated coast;
Oaks no more are riv'n in splinters
 By the whirlwind and his host.

Spinks and ouzles sing sublimely,
 'We too have a Saviour born,'
Whiter blossoms burst untimely
 On the blest Mosaic thorn.

God all-bounteous, all-creative,
 Whom no ills from good dissuade,
Is incarnate, and a native
 Of the very world he made.

THE WORKS OF HORACE, TRANSLATED INTO VERSE
London, 1767 [text].

From *Horace His Art of Poetry*
 . . .
 The true professor of the muse
 Shou'd know to take and to refuse;
 Yet if new words he intersperse,
 He shou'd be cautious in his verse,
 And choice—It is exceeding well
 To give a common word the *spell*,
 To greet you as intirely new—
 It is a point you must persue,
 In modern language to confirm
 Each strange and philosophic term,
 Words you may use, to ancient Rome

Unknown, yet modestly presume.
  But new coin'd words will ever be
Of more approv'd authority,
If from the Grecian fount they fall,
And their mutation be but small,
For why shou'd Rome Cæcilius give,
And Plautus a prerogative,
Which they to Virgil still deny,
And Varius?—Why may not e'en I
Make some improvements if I can,
Nor suffer from th' invidious clan,
Since Ennius and Cato's phrase
Their native tongue enrich and raise,
And terms exotic introduce—
All have, and must allow the use
To make a word, that cleanly chimes,
Stampt with th' impression of the times.
As when the leaves each fleeting year
Are chang'd—the earliest dis-appear
The first; our words in likewise fare,
The oldest perish, as it were,
And those new-coin'd are now in flow'r,
Like youths, in all their strength and pow'r.
. . .

  Words shall revive that now are gone,
And some, which most are look'd upon,
Shall perish, if dame fashion will,
Who has in her dominion still
Supreme prescriptive pow'r to teach
All written and colloquial speech.
. . .

  'Tis arduous common things to say
In such a clean peculiar way,
Untill they fairly seem your own.
. . .

Ode 1.4.

To Sextius, a Person of Consular Dignity

By describing the delightfulness of spring, and urging the common lot of mortality, he exhorts Sextius, as an Epicurean, to a life of voluptuousness.

> A Grateful change! Favonius, and the spring
> > To the sharp winter's keener blasts succeed.
> Along the beach, with ropes, the ships they bring,
> > And launch again, their watry way to speed.
> No more the plowmen in their cots delight,
> > Nor cattle are contented in the stall;
> No more the fields with hoary frosts are white,
> > But Cytherean Venus leads the ball.
> She, while the moon attends upon the scene,
> > The Nymphs and decent Graces in the set,
> Shakes with alternate feet the shaven green,
> > While Vulcan's Cyclops at the anvil sweat.
> Now we with myrtle shou'd adorn our brows,
> > Or any flow'r that decks the loosen'd sod;
> In shady groves to Faunus pay our vows,
> > Whether a lamb or kid delight the God.
> Pale death alike knocks at the poor man's door,
> > O happy Sextius, and the royal dome,
> The whole of life forbids our hope to soar,
> > Death and the shades anon shall press thee home.
> And when into the shallow grave you run,
> > You cannot win the monarchy of wine,
> Nor doat on Lycidas, as on a son,
> > Whom for their spouse all little maids design.

Ode 1. 25.

To Lydia

He insults her, that now being old, she is deservedly contemned by her gallants.

> More sparing the young rakes alarm
> > The window-shutters of their toast,
> You now may sleep secure of harm;

The door affects the post,
Which mov'd so oft its pliant hinge—
—You hear that serenade no more,
'Sleep'st thou, while dying lovers winge,
    O Lydia, at thy door!'
Jilt, thou the scoffing sparks shalt soon
    Lament, neglected in a lane,
When, at the changing of the moon,
    The north-west blows amain;
While love and vehement desire,
    Such as the mares for stallions seize,
Shall set your blister'd breast afire,
    Join'd to complaints like these,
That gladsome youths on ivy green
    And constant myrtle rather glote;
To Hebrus winter's comrade keen,
    The wither'd leaves devote.

Ode 1.38.

To his Servant

He would have him bring nothing for the gracing of his banquet but myrtle. In the original metre exactly.

Persian pomps, boy, ever I renounce them:
Scoff o' the plaited coronet's refulgence;
Seek not in fruitless vigilance the rose-tree's
    Tardier offspring.
Mere honest myrtle that alone is order'd,
Me the mere myrtle decorates, as also
Thee the prompt waiter to a jolly toper
    Hous'd in an arbour.

Ode 2.16.

To Grosphus

All men covet peace of mind, which cannot be acquired either by riches or honours, but only by restraining the appetites.

When o'er the Ægean vast he sails
    The seaman sues the gods for ease,
Soon as the moon the tempest veils,

Nor sparkling guide he sees.
Ease by fierce Thracians in the end;
  Ease by the quiver'd Mede is sought;
By gems, nor purple bales, my friend,
  Nor bullion to be bought.
Not wealth or state, a consul's share,
  Can give the troubled mind its rest,
Or fray the winged fiends of care,
  That pompous roofs infest.
Well lives he, on whose little board
  Th' old silver salt-cellar appears,
Left by his sires—no sordid hoard
  Disturb his sleep with fears.
Why with such strength of thought devise,
  And aim at sublunary pelf,
Seek foreign realms? Can he, who flies
  His country, 'scape himself?
Ill-natur'd care will board the fleet,
  Nor leave the squadron'd troops behind,
Swifter than harts, or irksome sleet
  Driv'n by the eastern wind.
If good, the present hour be mirth;
  If bitter, let your smiles be sweet,
Look not too forward—nought on earth
  Is in all points complete.
A sudden death Achilles seiz'd,
  A tedious age Tithonus wore—
If you're amerc'd, fate may be pleas'd
  To give to me the more.
A hundred flocks around thee stray,
  About thee low Sicilian kine,
And mares apt for thy carriage neigh,
  And purple robes are thine.
Me, born for verse and rural peace,
  A faithful prophetess foretold,
And groundlings, spirited from Greece,
  In high contempt I hold.

Ode 2.18.

He asserts himself to be contented with a little fortune, where others labour for wealth, and the gratification of their desires, as if they were to live for ever.

> Gold or iv'ry's not intended
>   For this little house of mine,
> Nor Hymettian arches, bended
>   On rich Afric pillars, shine.
> For a court I've no ambition,
>   As not Attalus his heir,
> Nor make damsels of condition
>   Spin me purple for my wear.
> But for truth and wit respected,
>   I possess a copious vein,
> So that rich men have affected
>   To be number'd of my train.
> With my Sabine field contented,
>   Fortune shall be dunn'd no more;
> Nor my gen'rous friend tormented
>   To augment my little store.
> One day by the next's abolish'd,
>   Moons increase but to decay;
> You place marbles to be polish'd
>   Ev'n upon your dying day.
> Death unheeding, though infirmer,
>   On the sea your buildings rise,
> While the Baian billows murmur,
>   That the land will not suffice.
> What tho' more and more incroaching,
>   On new boundaries you press,
> And in avarice approaching,
>   Your poor neighbours dispossess;
> The griev'd hind his gods displaces,
>   In his bosom to convey,
> And with dirty ruddy faces
>   Boys and wife are driven away.
> Yet no palace grand and spacious

Does more sure its lord receive,
Than the seat of death rapacious,
   Whence the rich have no reprieve.
Earth alike to all is equal,
   Whither would your views extend?
Kings and peasants in the sequel
   To the destin'd grave descend.
There, tho' brib'd, the guard infernal
   Would not shrewd Promotheus free;
There are held in chains eternal
   Tantalus, and such as he.
There the poor have consolation
   For their hard laborious lot;
Death attends each rank and station,
   Whether he is call'd or not.

Ode 3.22.
To Diana
*He consecrates the pine, which hangs over his villa, to Diana,
whose offices he celebrates.*

Queen of the mountains far and near,
   And of the woodlands wild,
Who, thrice invok'd, art swift to hear,
   And save the maids with child;
This pine, that o'er my villa tow'rs,
And from its eminence embow'rs,
   I dedicate alone to thee;
Where ev'ry year a pig shall bleed,
Lest his obliquity succeed
   Against thy fav'rite tree.

Ode 4.2.
To Antonius Julus, the Son of Mark Antony, of the Triumvirate
It is hazardous to imitate the ancient poets.

Whoever vies with Pindar's strain,
   With waxen wings, my friend, would fly,
Like him who nam'd the glassy main,

But could not reach the sky.
Cascading from the mountain's height,
   As falls the river swoln with show'rs,
Deep, fierce, and out of measure great
      His verses Pindar pours.
Worthy to claim Apollo's bays,
   Whether his dithyrambics roll,
Daring their new-invented phrase
      And words, that scorn controul.
Or gods he chants, or kings, the seed
   Of gods, who rose to virtuous fame,
And justly Centaurs doom'd to bleed,
      Or quench'd Chimera's flame.
Or champions of th' Elean justs,
   The wrestler, charioteer records,
And, better than a hundred busts,
      He gives divine rewards.
Snatch'd from his weeping bride, the youth
   His verse deplores, and will display
Strength, courage, and his golden truth,
      And grudges death his prey.
The Theban swan ascends with haste,
   Of heav'n's superior regions free;
But I, exactly in the taste
      Of some Matinian bee,
That hardly gets the thymy spoil
   About moist Tibur's flow'ry ways,
Of small account, with tedious toil,
      Compose my labour'd lays.
You, bard indeed! with more applause
   Shall Cæsar sing, so justly crown'd,
As up the sacred hill he draws
      The fierce Sicambrians bound.
A greater and a better gift
   Than him, from heav'n we do not hold,
Nor shall—although the times should shift
      Into their pristine gold.

The festal days and public sports
    For our brave chief's returning here,
You shall recite, and all the courts
    Of law contentions clear.
Then would I speak to ears like thine,
    With no small portion of my voice,
O glorious day! O most divine!
    Which Cæsar bids rejoice.
And while you in procession hie,
    Hail triumph! triumph! will we shout
All Rome—and our good gods supply
    With frankincense devout!
Thee bulls and heifers ten suffice—
    Me a calf weaned from the cow,
At large who many a gambol tries,
    Though doom'd to pay my vow.
Like the new moon, upon his crest
    He wears a semicircle bright,
His body yellow all the rest,
    Except this spot of white.

Ode 4.7.

To L. Manlius Torquatus

All things are changed by time; one ought therefore to live chearfully.

The melted snow the verdure now restores,
    And leaves adorn the trees;
The season shifts—subsiding to their shores
    The rivers flow with ease.
The Grace, with nymphs and with her sisters twain,
    Tho' naked dares the dance—
That here's no permanence the years explain,
    And days, as they advance.
The air grows mild with zephyrs, as the spring
    To summer cedes the sway,
Which flies when autumn hastes his fruits to bring,
    Then winter comes in play.

The moons their heav'nly damages supply—
    Not so the mortal star—
Where good Eneas, Tullus, Ancus lie,
    Ashes and dust we are.
Who knows if heav'n will give to-morrow's boon
    To this our daily pray'r?
The goods you take to keep your soul in tune,
    Shall scape your greedy heir.
When you shall die, tho' Minos must acquit
    A part so nobly play'd;
Race, eloquence, and goodness, from the pit
    Cannot restore your shade.
For nor Diana's heav'nly pow'r or love,
    Hippolytus revives;
Nor Theseus can Perithous remove
    From his Lethean gives.

The Secular Ode
For the safety of the Roman empire.

    Phoebus and Dian, queen of bow'rs,
        Bright grace of Heav'n, the things we pray;
    O most adorable of pow'rs,
    And still by adoration ours,
        Grant us this sacred day.

    At which the Sybils in their song
        Ingenuous youths and virgins warn;
    Selected from the vulgar throng,
    The gods, to whom sev'n hills belong,
        With verses to adorn.

    O fost'ring god, whose fall or flame,
        Can hide the day or re-illume;
    Which com'st another and the same,
    May'st thou see nothing like the fame,
        And magnitude of Rome!

And thou, to whom the pray'r's preferr'd,
   The matrons in their throes to ease;
O let our vows in time be heard,
Whether Lucina be the word,
     Or genial goddess please.

Make fruitful ev'ry nuptial bed,
   And bless the conscript father's scheme,
Enjoining bloomy maids to wed,
And let the marriage-bill be sped,
     With a new race to teem.

That years elev'n times ten come round,
   These sports and songs of grave delight;
Thrice by bright day-light may resound,
And where the thickest crouds abound,
     Thrice in the welcome night.

And you, ye destinies, sincere
   To sing what good our realm awaits;
Let peace establish'd persevere,
And add to them, which now appear,
     Still hope of better fates.

Let fertile earth, for flocks and fruit,
   Greet Ceres with a wheaten crown;
And ev'ry youngling, sprout, and shoot,
Let Jove with air attemper'd suit,
     While wholesome rains come down.

Serene, as when your darts you sheathe,
   Phœbus, the suppliant youths befriend;
And all the vows the virgins breathe,
Up to thy crescent from beneath,
     Thou, queen of stars, attend.

If Rome be yours, and if a band
   Of Trojans safely came by sea;
To coast upon th' Etrurian strand,
And change their city and their land,
     By your supreme decree.

For whom, unhurt, thro' burning Troy
   The chaste Æneas way cou'd find;
He whom the foes could not destroy,
But liv'd to make his friends enjoy,
     More than they left behind.

—Ye gods, our youth in morals train,
   With sweet repose old age solace;
On Rome, in general, O rain
All circumstance, increase, and gain,
     Each glory and each grace.

And he whose beeves were milky white,
   When to your shrine his pray'rs appeal'd;
Of Venus and Anchises hight,
O let him reign supreme in fight,
     But mild to them that yield.

By sea and land, the Parthians now
   Our arms and ax with dread review;
For terms of peace the Scythians bow,
And, lately arrogant of brow,
     To us the Indians sue.

Now public faith and honour dare,
   With ancient modesty and peace;
To show their heads, and virtue rare,
And she that's wont her horn to bear,
     With plentiful increase.

The archer with his shining bow,
      The seer that wins each muse's heart;
Phœbus, who respite can bestow,
To limbs in weakness and in woe,
          By his salubrious art.

If, built on Palatine, the height
      Of his own towrs his eyes engage;
The Roman and the Latian state,
Extend he to a longer date,
          And still a better age!

And may Diana, who controuls
      Mount Algidus and Aventine;
To those great men that keep the rolls,
And to the youths that lift their souls,
          A gracious ear incline!

That Jove, and all the gods, will bless
      Our pray'rs, good hope my thoughts forebode;
THE CHORUS, who such skill possess,
Phœbus and Dian to address,
          In this thanksgiving ode.

Lyrics from ABIMELECH, AN ORATORIO
London, 1768 [text].
Part 2, p. 11.
      There is no rose to minds in grief;
          There is no lilly for despair;
      Tears and distraction are relief,
          And yews and willows we must wear.

      All nature's blandishments are vain
          From flow'ry turf, or azure sky,
      And grottoes, where the groans of pain
          In sadly sounding echoes die.

Part 2, p. 12.

Tho' yon tall almond blooms no more,
'Tis not because its sweets are o'er
   On each aspiring shoot—
Attend to what the starlings sing,
Another year, another spring,
The buds to gayer pride shall bring,
   It now prepares for fruit.

HYMNS FOR THE AMUSEMENT OF CHILDREN
1770. Third edition London, 1775 [text].

Hymn XII
Honesty

I have a house, the house of prayer,
   (No spy beneath my eaves)
And purring gratitude is there,
   And he that frights the thieves.

If I of honesty suspend
   My judgment, making doubt,
I have a good domestic friend,
   That soon shall point it out.

'Tis to be faithful to my charge,
   And thankful for my place,
And pray that God my pow'rs enlarge,
   To act with greater grace.

To give my brother more than due,
   In talent or in name;
Nor e'en mine enemy pursue,
   To hurt or to defame.

Nay more, to bless him and to pray,
   Mine anger to controul;
And give the wages of the day
   To him that hunts my soul.

Hymn XXI
Generosity

That vast communicative mind,
That form'd the world and human kind,
  And saw that all was right;
Or was thyself, or came from Thee,
Stupendous generosity,
  Above all lustre bright.

'Not *for themselves the bees prepare
Their honey, and the fleecy care,
  Not for themselves are shorn:
Not for themselves the warblers build,
Not for themselves the lands are till'd,
  By them that tread the corn.'

The Lord shed on the Holy Rood
His infinitely gen'rous blood,
  Not for himself, but all;
Yea, e'en for them that pierc'd his side,
In patient agony he died,
  To remedy the fall.

O highly rais'd above the ranks
Of Angels—he cou'd e'en give thanks,
  Self-rais'd and self-renew'd—
Then who can praise, and love, and fear
Enough?—since he himself, 'tis clear,
  Is also gratitude.

---

*Virgil. [Smart].

Hymn XXII
Gratitude

I upon the first creation
  Clap'd my wings with loud applause,
Cherub of the highest station,
  Praising, blessing, without pause.

I in Eden's bloomy bowers
    Was the heav'nly gardner's pride,
Sweet of sweets, and flow'r of flowers,
    With the scented tinctures dy'd.

Hear, ye little children, hear me,
    I am God's delightful voice;
They who sweetly still revere me,
    Still shall make the wisest choice.

Hear me not like Adam trembling,
    When I walk'd in Eden's grove;
And the host of heav'n assembling,
    From the spot the traitor drove.

Hear me rather as the lover
    Of mankind, restor'd and free;
By the word ye shall recover
    More than that ye lost by Me.

I'm the Phœnix of the singers,
    That in upper Eden dwell;
Hearing me Euphrates lingers,
    As my wondrous tale I tell.

'Tis the story of the Graces,
    Mercies without end or sum;
And the sketches and the traces
    Of ten thousand more to come.

List, my children, list within you,
    Dread not ye the tempter's rod;
Christ our gratitude shall win you,
    Wean'd from earth, and led to God.

Hymn XXV
Mirth

If you are merry sing away,
    And touch the organs sweet;
This is the Lord's triumphant day,
Ye children in the gall'ries gay,
    Shout from each goodly seat.

It shall be May to-morrow's morn,
    A field then let us run,
And deck us in the blooming thorn,
Soon as the cock begins to warn,
    And long before the sun.

I give the praise to Christ alone,
    My pinks already shew;
And my streak'd roses fully blown,
The sweetness of the Lord make known,
    And to his glory grow.

Ye little prattlers that repair
    For cowslips in the mead,
Of those exulting colts beware,
But blythe security is there,
    Where skipping lambkins feed.

With white and crimson laughs the sky,
    With birds the hedge-rows ring;
To give the praise to God most high,
And all the sulky fiends defy,
    Is a most joyful thing.

Hymn XXXII
Against Despair
Old Ralph in the Wood

> A Raven once an Acorn took
> > From Bashan's tallest stoutest tree;
> He hid it by a limpid brook,
> > And liv'd another oak to see.

> Thus Melancholy buries Hope,
> > Which Providence keeps still alive,
> And bids us with afflictions cope,
> > And all anxiety survive.

Hymn XXXIII
For Saturday

> Now's the time for mirth and play,
> Saturday's an holiday;
> Praise to heav'n unceasing yield,
> I've found a lark's nest in the field.

> A lark's nest, then your play-mate begs
> You'd spare herself and speckled eggs;
> Soon she shall ascend and sing
> Your praises to th' eternal King.

Hymn XXXIV
For Sunday

> Arise—arise—the Lord arose
> > On this triumphant day;
> Your soul to piety dispose,
> > Arise to bless and pray.

> Ev'n rustics do adorn them now,
> > Themselves in roses dress;
> And to the clergyman they bow,
> > When he begins to bless.

Their best apparel now arrays
    The little girls and boys;
And better than the preacher prays
    For heav'n's eternal joys.